HOW TO GET A JOB IN TECH AND IT

Proven Strategies for Landing a Dream Job in Technology and IT

Thomas Gray

Copyright © 2024 by Thomas Gray

All rights reserved.
No part of this work may be reproduced, distributed, or transmitted in any form or by any means, including photocopying, recording, or other electronic or mechanical methods, without the prior written permission of the copyright holder, except in the case of brief quotations embodied in critical reviews and certain other noncommercial uses permitted by copyright law.

Table of Contents

Introduction to the Tech and IT Job Market   5

Chapter 1: Understanding Key Trends in Technology and IT   12

Chapter 2: Essential Skills for Tech and IT Careers 22

Chapter 3: Building a Strong Tech and IT Resume 33

Chapter 4: Crafting an Effective Cover Letter for IT Jobs   42

Chapter 5: Optimizing Your LinkedIn Profile for Tech Recruiters   50

Chapter 6: Networking Strategies for IT Professionals   59

Chapter 7: Mastering the Tech Job Application Process   68

Chapter 8: Preparing for Technical Interviews in IT 77

Chapter 9: Common Tech and IT Interview

Questions and How to Answer Them   88

Chapter 10: Technical Skills Assessment and Coding Tests   99

Chapter 11: Showcasing Your Tech Projects and Portfolio   110

Chapter 12: Leveraging Certifications in the Tech Industry   120

Chapter 13: Understanding Different Tech Job Roles and Their Requirements   131

Chapter 14: Salary Negotiation Tips for IT Professionals   141

Chapter 15: Working with Tech Recruiters and Staffing Agencies   150

Chapter 16: Freelancing and Contract Work in Technology   162

Chapter 17: Continuing Education and Professional Development in IT   175

Chapter 18: Remote Work Opportunities in Tech   188

Chapter 19: Balancing Work and Life in a Tech Career   **203**

Chapter 20: Future Trends in Technology and IT Careers   **214**

Conclusion   **225**

Introduction to the Tech and IT Job Market

If you are reading this, you are probably interested in starting or advancing your career in the exciting field of technology and IT. The tech and IT job market is growing quickly, offering many opportunities for people with the right skills and enthusiasm.

The Rapid Growth of Tech and IT
The tech industry is one of the fastest-growing areas in the global economy. From startups to large corporations, companies are investing heavily in technology. This growth is driven by advances in areas like artificial intelligence, cybersecurity, cloud computing, and data science. Because of this, there is a high demand for skilled professionals who can help businesses stay competitive and innovative.

IT is essential to almost every modern organization. It includes maintaining computer systems and networks, developing software, and ensuring data security. With more reliance on digital solutions, the need for IT professionals is greater than ever.

Why a Career in Tech and IT?

There are many reasons why a career in tech and IT is appealing:

1. High Demand: There are always job opportunities in tech and IT, which means better job security.

2. Good Salaries: Tech and IT jobs often come with good pay and benefits, even for entry-level positions.

3. Innovation: If you enjoy solving problems and working with new technologies, this field is for you. There are always new challenges and opportunities to learn.

4. Diverse Opportunities: Whether you like coding, network security, data analysis, or project management, there is a place for you in tech and IT. The field is diverse and offers roles that match different interests and skills.

5. Flexibility: Many tech and IT jobs offer flexible working options, including remote work. This can help you balance work and personal life.

6. Impact: Working in tech and IT allows you to make a real difference. You can create solutions that improve lives, enhance business operations, and contribute to progress.

The Changing Landscape of Tech Jobs
The tech and IT job market changes rapidly with new technologies and industry trends. Here are some current trends:

- Artificial Intelligence (AI) and Machine Learning (ML): These technologies are transforming industries from healthcare to finance. Professionals with AI and ML skills are in high demand.

- Cybersecurity: With more cyber threats, cybersecurity is a top priority for organizations, leading to a surge in demand for cybersecurity experts.

- Cloud Computing: More businesses are moving their operations to the cloud, creating a need for cloud specialists.

- Data Science and Analytics: Data is very valuable. Companies need data scientists to interpret large amounts of data for better business decisions.

- Remote Work Technology: The increase in remote work has led to the development of tools and platforms that support virtual collaboration and productivity.

Preparing for a Tech and IT Career

Starting a career in tech and IT requires preparation and dedication. Here are some steps to help you:

1. Education: A degree in computer science or a related field is helpful but not always necessary. Many tech professionals are self-taught or have attended coding boot camps.

2. Skills Development: Build both technical and soft skills. Technical skills might include programming languages, systems administration, or cybersecurity. Soft skills, like communication and problem-solving, are also important.

3. Certifications: Getting industry-recognized certifications can enhance your credibility and job prospects. Examples include CompTIA, AWS, and Cisco certifications.

4. Networking: Connect with other professionals through networking events, online communities, and platforms like LinkedIn.

5. Portfolio: Create a portfolio to showcase your projects and skills. This can be a personal website, a GitHub repository, or a collection of case studies.

6. Stay Updated: The tech industry changes quickly. Keep up with the latest trends, tools, and technologies by reading industry blogs, attending webinars, and participating in professional development opportunities.

The tech and IT job market offers many opportunities for those willing to learn and grow. With the right approach, you can build a successful and fulfilling career in this dynamic field. This book will guide you through the essential steps to land your dream job in technology and IT.

Chapter 1: Understanding Key Trends in Technology and IT

The world of technology and IT is always changing. Keeping up with these changes is important if you want to have a successful career in this field. In this chapter, we will look at some key trends that are shaping the future of technology and IT. Understanding these trends will help you stay ahead of the curve and make informed decisions about your career.

Artificial Intelligence (AI) and Machine Learning (ML)

Artificial Intelligence (AI) and Machine Learning (ML) are two of the most exciting areas in tech today. AI refers to the ability of machines to perform tasks that would normally require human intelligence, such as understanding natural language or recognizing patterns. ML is a subset of AI that involves training machines to learn from data and improve over time.

These technologies are being used in many different industries. For example, in healthcare, AI can help doctors diagnose diseases more accurately. In finance, ML algorithms can predict stock market trends. Companies are looking for professionals who can develop and implement AI and ML solutions. If you have skills in this area, you will be in high demand.

Cybersecurity

As more of our lives move online, cybersecurity has become more important than ever. Cybersecurity involves protecting computers, networks, and data from unauthorized access or attacks. With the rise in cyber threats, companies are investing heavily in cybersecurity measures.

Cybersecurity professionals are needed to identify vulnerabilities, develop security protocols, and respond to security breaches. If you have skills in this area, you can help organizations protect their valuable information. This field offers many opportunities for growth and specialization.

Cloud Computing
Cloud computing is another major trend in tech. It involves delivering computing services—such as storage, processing, and networking—over the internet (the cloud). This allows businesses to scale their operations quickly and efficiently.
Many companies are moving their operations to the cloud because it offers flexibility and cost savings. Cloud specialists are needed to manage these services and ensure they run smoothly. Skills in cloud platforms like Amazon Web Services (AWS), Microsoft Azure, and Google Cloud are highly valued in the job market.

Data Science and Analytics
Data is often called the new oil because it is so valuable. Companies collect vast amounts of data, and they need professionals who can make sense of it. Data science involves using

statistical methods and algorithms to analyze data and extract useful insights.

Data analysts and data scientists are in high demand. They help businesses make informed decisions, improve operations, and understand customer behavior. If you enjoy working with numbers and have strong analytical skills, a career in data science could be very rewarding.

Internet of Things (IoT)

The Internet of Things (IoT) refers to the network of physical devices—such as cars, appliances, and sensors—that are connected to the internet and can communicate with each other. IoT is transforming industries like manufacturing, healthcare, and transportation.

For example, in smart homes, IoT devices can control lighting, heating, and security systems remotely. In agriculture, IoT sensors can monitor soil conditions and optimize irrigation. Professionals who can develop and manage IoT systems are in high demand as this technology continues to grow.

Blockchain

Blockchain is a technology that allows for secure and transparent transactions without the need for a central authority. It is best known as the technology behind cryptocurrencies like Bitcoin, but it has many other applications.

For instance, blockchain can be used for supply chain management, ensuring that products are sourced and delivered as expected. It can also be used for secure voting systems and digital identity verification. Skills in blockchain development and implementation are becoming increasingly valuable.

Augmented Reality (AR) and Virtual Reality (VR)

Augmented Reality (AR) and Virtual Reality (VR) are technologies that create immersive experiences. AR overlays digital information onto the real world, while VR creates a completely virtual environment.

These technologies are being used in various fields, such as gaming, education, and healthcare. For example, in education, AR can bring textbooks to life with interactive content. In healthcare, VR can be used for surgical training and therapy. Professionals with skills in AR and VR development are needed to create these innovative solutions.

Automation and Robotics

Automation and robotics are transforming the way we work. Automation involves using technology to perform tasks that would otherwise require human intervention. Robotics involves creating machines that can perform physical tasks.

These technologies are being used in industries like manufacturing, logistics, and healthcare. For example, robots can assemble products on a factory floor, while automated systems can manage inventory in a warehouse. Skills in automation and robotics can open up many career opportunities.

Edge Computing

Edge computing is a trend that involves processing data closer to where it is generated, rather than sending it to a central server. This can reduce latency and improve efficiency, especially for applications that require real-time processing.

For example, self-driving cars need to process data from sensors in real-time to navigate safely. Edge computing enables this by processing data locally. As more devices become connected, the need for edge computing professionals will continue to grow.

5G Technology
5G is the next generation of mobile network technology. It offers faster speeds, lower latency, and greater capacity than previous generations. This will enable new applications and services, such as enhanced mobile broadband, massive IoT deployments, and real-time communication for autonomous vehicles.

As 5G networks are deployed worldwide, there will be a growing demand for professionals who can design, implement, and manage these networks. Understanding 5G technology and its potential applications can give you a competitive edge in the job market.

The tech and IT job market is constantly evolving with new trends and technologies. Understanding these key trends can help you stay informed and make better career choices. Whether you are just starting out or looking to advance your career, staying updated with the latest developments in technology and IT will position you for success. This chapter has covered some of the most important trends shaping the future of this dynamic field. By focusing on these areas, you can build a rewarding career and make a significant impact in the tech world.

Chapter 2: Essential Skills for Tech and IT Careers

Entering the world of technology and IT can be exciting and rewarding. To succeed in this field, you need to develop a mix of technical and soft skills. In this chapter, we'll explore the essential skills you need for a successful career in tech and IT. Whether you're a beginner or looking to advance, mastering these skills will help you stand out in a competitive job market.

Technical Skills

1. Programming Languages
Learning to code is fundamental for many tech jobs. Programming languages are the tools you use to write software and develop applications. Some popular languages include:

- Python: Great for beginners, Python is widely used in web development, data science, and automation.
- JavaScript: Essential for web development, JavaScript allows you to create interactive websites.
- Java: Used in many large-scale applications, including Android apps and enterprise software.
- C++: Known for its performance, C++ is used in game development and systems programming.

Pick one or two languages to start with and practice regularly. Online resources, coding boot camps, and courses can help you learn and improve.

2. Understanding Algorithms and Data Structures

Algorithms and data structures are the building blocks of efficient software. They help you solve problems quickly and use computer resources effectively. Common data structures include arrays, linked lists, and hash tables. Algorithms like sorting and searching are crucial for handling data. Understanding these concepts will improve your coding skills and make you a better problem solver.

3. Web Development

Knowing how to build websites is a valuable skill. Web development involves creating the structure, design, and functionality of websites. Key skills include:

  - HTML/CSS: The basics of web development, used to structure and style web pages.
  - Responsive Design: Ensuring websites work well on all devices, from desktops to smartphones.
  - Frameworks: Tools like React, Angular, and Vue.js help streamline web development and make it more efficient.

4. Database Management

Databases store and organize data, which is essential for most applications. Skills in database management include:

- SQL: The standard language for querying and managing databases.
- NoSQL: Databases like MongoDB and Cassandra are used to handle unstructured data.
- Database Design: Understanding how to structure data and create efficient database schemas.

5. Networking

Networking involves connecting computers and devices to share resources and information. Key concepts include:

- IP Addressing: Understanding how devices are identified on a network.
- Routing and Switching: How data is transferred across networks.
- Network Security: Protecting networks from unauthorized access and cyber threats.

6. Operating Systems

Knowing how to use and manage operating systems is crucial. Common operating systems include:

 - Windows: Widely used in business environments.
 - Linux: Popular for servers and development due to its stability and security.
 - macOS: Used by many developers and creative professionals.

Understanding file systems, process management, and system commands will make you more versatile.

7. Cloud Computing

Cloud computing involves delivering computing services over the Internet. Key skills include:

 - Cloud Platforms: Familiarity with platforms like AWS, Microsoft Azure, and Google Cloud.
 - Deployment and Management: Knowing how to deploy and manage applications in the cloud.
 - Scalability: Ensuring applications can handle increased demand by scaling resources.

8. Cybersecurity

Protecting systems and data from threats is critical. Important skills include:

- Threat Detection: Identifying potential security threats and vulnerabilities.
- Incident Response: Responding to and mitigating security breaches.
- Security Protocols: Implementing security measures like encryption and firewalls.

Soft Skills

1. Problem-Solving

Tech professionals often face complex problems that require creative solutions. Being able to break down problems, analyze them, and find effective solutions is crucial. Practice solving different types of problems and think about how you approach challenges.

2. Communication

Clear communication is important in tech and IT. You need to explain technical concepts to non-technical people, write documentation, and work with team members. Improve your written and verbal communication skills by practicing regularly and seeking feedback.

3. Teamwork

Many tech projects involve working with others. Being a good team player means collaborating, sharing ideas, and supporting your teammates. Work on your ability to cooperate and contribute positively to a team environment.

4. Time Management

Tech projects often have tight deadlines. Managing your time effectively ensures you complete tasks on schedule. Use tools like calendars, task lists, and project management software to stay organized and prioritize your work.

5. Adaptability

The tech industry changes quickly. Being adaptable means staying open to new ideas, learning new skills, and adjusting to changes. Keep up with industry trends and be willing to step out of your comfort zone.

6. Attention to Detail
In tech and IT, small mistakes can lead to big problems. Paying close attention to detail helps you avoid errors and produce high-quality work. Double-check your code, review your work, and develop a habit of thoroughness.

How to Develop These Skills

1. Education and Training
Formal education, like a degree in computer science or IT, can provide a solid foundation. However, many successful tech professionals are self-taught or have attended coding boot camps. Online courses, tutorials, and books are excellent resources for learning new skills.

2. Practice and Projects

Practice is key to mastering technical skills. Work on personal projects, contribute to open-source projects or take on freelance work. Building a portfolio of your work can showcase your skills to potential employers.

3. Certifications
Certifications can validate your skills and knowledge. Consider certifications from recognized organizations, such as:

- CompTIA: Offers certifications in areas like IT fundamentals, networking, and security.
- AWS: Certifications for different levels of expertise in cloud computing.
- Cisco: Networking certifications, including CCNA and CCNP.

4. Networking
Connect with other professionals in the field. Attend industry events, join online communities, and participate in forums. Networking can provide support, mentorship, and job opportunities.

5. Stay Updated

The tech industry evolves rapidly. Stay informed about the latest trends, tools, and technologies by reading blogs, following industry news, and participating in webinars and conferences.

Developing the essential skills for a tech and IT career requires dedication and continuous learning. By mastering both technical and soft skills, you can position yourself for success in this dynamic field. This chapter has highlighted the key skills you need and provided tips on how to develop them. Focus on building these skills, and you'll be well-prepared to pursue a rewarding career in technology and IT.

Chapter 3: Building a Strong Tech and IT Resume

Creating a strong resume is essential for landing a job in the tech and IT field. Your resume is often the first impression you make on a potential employer, so it's important to make it count. In this chapter, we'll explore how to craft a resume that stands out, highlights your skills, and gets you noticed by hiring managers.

Understanding the Basics
A good resume should be clear, concise, and easy to read. Start with a clean, professional layout. Use a simple font and avoid excessive formatting. Your goal is to make it easy for the employer to quickly see your qualifications.

Begin with your contact information at the top of the page. Include your name, phone number, email address, and LinkedIn profile. Make sure your email address is professional—ideally just your name.

Crafting a Compelling Summary
The summary section is your elevator pitch. It's a brief statement at the top of your resume that highlights your experience and what you bring to the table. Keep it short, about 2-3 sentences, and focus on your key strengths and what makes you unique.

For example, "Experienced software developer with 5 years in full-stack development. Skilled in Python, JavaScript, and cloud computing. Passionate about building scalable web applications and improving user experience."

Highlighting Your Experience
Your work experience section should include your job titles, company names, locations, and dates of employment. For each position, provide a few bullet points that describe your responsibilities and achievements. Focus on quantifiable results—specific accomplishments that demonstrate your skills and impact.

For example:
- Developed and maintained a web application that increased user engagement by 30%.
- Led a team of 5 developers to deliver a major project on time and under budget.
- Implemented a new feature that reduced load times by 50%.

Use action verbs like "developed," "led," "implemented," and "improved" to make your achievements sound dynamic and impactful.

Emphasizing Your Skills

The skills section is crucial for a tech and IT resume. List your technical skills first, including programming languages, tools, and technologies you are proficient in. Be specific and honest about your proficiency level—don't list a skill unless you are comfortable using it.

You might also include a section for soft skills, such as teamwork, communication, and problem-solving. These are important in any job and show that you're well-rounded.

For example:
- Technical Skills: Python, JavaScript, HTML/CSS, SQL, AWS, Docker
- Soft Skills: Team collaboration, project management, effective communication, critical thinking

Showcasing Your Education

List your educational background, including your degrees, institutions, and graduation dates. If you have relevant coursework or honors, include those as well. For recent graduates, you might place this section near the top of your resume. For more experienced professionals, it can go toward the bottom.

If you've attended coding boot camps, online courses, or earned certifications, list these in a separate section called "Certifications and Training." This shows your commitment to continuous learning and staying updated with industry trends.

Including Projects and Portfolio

Projects are a great way to showcase your skills, especially if you're new to the field or changing careers. Include a section for projects where you describe personal or professional projects relevant to the job you're applying for.

For each project, provide a brief description of the technologies used, and your role in the project. If possible, include links to your GitHub repository or a personal portfolio website where employers can see your work.

For example:
- E-commerce Website: Developed a full-stack e-commerce website using React, Node.js, and MongoDB. Implemented user authentication, payment processing, and product management features. (Link to GitHub)
- Chat Application: Created a real-time chat application using WebSocket, Express.js, and Bootstrap. Enabled user-to-user messaging and group chats. (Link to GitHub)

Tailoring Your Resume

One of the most important aspects of building a strong resume is tailoring it to each job application. Review the job description carefully and highlight the skills and experiences that match the requirements. Use keywords from the job posting in your resume to increase the chances of passing through Applicant Tracking Systems (ATS).

If a job emphasizes certain skills, make sure those skills are prominently featured on your resume. Customize your summary, work experience, and skills sections to align with the specific job.

Proofreading and Feedback

Before submitting your resume, proofread it carefully to catch any errors. Spelling mistakes or grammatical errors can make a bad impression. Use tools like Grammarly to help with this, and consider asking a friend or mentor to review your resume for feedback.

Make sure your resume is consistent in terms of formatting, font size, and style. A polished and professional-looking resume shows attention to detail.

Leveraging LinkedIn

Your LinkedIn profile complements your resume and can provide additional information about your experience and skills. Make sure your LinkedIn profile is up-to-date and matches the information on your resume. Include a professional photo, a compelling headline, and a detailed summary.

Join relevant LinkedIn groups, follow industry leaders, and engage with content to increase your visibility. Recommendations and endorsements from colleagues and supervisors can also enhance your profile.

Building a strong tech and IT resume requires effort and attention to detail, but it's worth it. A well-crafted resume can open doors to exciting job opportunities and help you advance your career. Focus on highlighting your relevant skills, experiences, and achievements in a clear and concise manner. Tailor your resume for each job application and make sure it's error-free.

With a strong resume in hand, you'll be well on your way to landing your dream job in technology and IT.

Chapter 4: Crafting an Effective Cover Letter for IT Jobs

Crafting an Effective Cover Letter for IT Jobs

A cover letter is a crucial part of your job application. It's your chance to make a personal connection with the hiring manager and explain why you're the best fit for the job. In this chapter, we'll guide you through crafting an effective cover letter for IT jobs that stands out and captures the attention of potential employers.

Understanding the Purpose of a Cover Letter

The main purpose of a cover letter is to introduce yourself and explain why you're interested in the position. It allows you to highlight your relevant skills and experiences in a way that complements your resume. A well-written cover letter can set you apart from other candidates and make a strong case for why you should be invited for an interview.

Starting with a Strong Opening

Begin your cover letter with a professional greeting. If possible, address it to a specific person, such as the hiring manager. This shows that you've done your research and are genuinely interested in the position. If you don't know the name of the hiring manager, a general greeting like "Dear Hiring Manager" is acceptable.

In your opening paragraph, introduce yourself and state the position you're applying for. Mention where you found the job posting and briefly explain why you're excited about the opportunity.

For example, "My name is Jane Doe, and I am writing to express my interest in the Software Developer position at Tech Solutions, as advertised on your website. With a strong background in full-stack development and a passion for creating innovative software solutions, I believe I am well-suited for this role."

Showcasing Your Skills and Experience
In the body of your cover letter, highlight your most relevant skills and experiences. Choose examples that demonstrate your ability to perform the job duties and contribute to the company's success. Focus on specific achievements and how they relate to the job you're applying for.

For instance, "In my previous role at XYZ Corp, I developed a web application that increased user engagement by 40%. Using technologies such as JavaScript, React, and Node.js, I led a team of developers to deliver the project on time and within budget. My experience in managing complex projects and collaborating with cross-functional teams has prepared me to excel in this position."

Aligning with the Company's Needs
Show that you understand the company's goals and how your skills can help them achieve those

goals. Tailor your cover letter to the specific job and company by researching their mission, values, and recent projects. This demonstrates your genuine interest and enthusiasm for the role.

For example, "I am particularly impressed with Tech Solutions' commitment to leveraging cutting-edge technology to solve real-world problems. Your recent project on developing AI-driven solutions for healthcare aligns with my experience and passion for using technology to improve lives. I am eager to contribute my expertise in machine learning and data analysis to further advance your innovative initiatives."

Demonstrating Your Enthusiasm

Employers want to hire candidates who are enthusiastic and motivated. Express your excitement for the role and the opportunity to work with the company. Explain why this job is a good fit for your career goals and how it aligns with your professional aspirations.

For instance, "Joining Tech Solutions represents an exciting step in my career. I am eager to work with a team of talented professionals and contribute to projects that make a meaningful impact. The opportunity to grow and learn in such an innovative environment is something I highly value."

Closing with Confidence

In your closing paragraph, reiterate your interest in the position and thank the hiring manager for considering your application. Express your willingness to discuss your application further and provide your contact information.

For example, "Thank you for considering my application. I am excited about the opportunity to bring my skills and experiences to Tech Solutions and contribute to your team's success. I look forward to the possibility of discussing how my background aligns with your needs in more detail. Please feel free to contact me at (your phone number) or via email at (your email address) to schedule an interview."

End with a professional closing, such as "Sincerely" or "Best regards," followed by your name.

Polishing Your Cover Letter

Before sending your cover letter, proofread it carefully to ensure there are no spelling or grammatical errors. A well-polished cover letter shows attention to detail and professionalism. Consider asking a friend or mentor to review it and provide feedback.

Make sure your cover letter is concise and to the point. Aim for a length of about one page. Use a professional tone and avoid overly casual language.

Crafting an effective cover letter for IT jobs requires thought and effort, but it can make a significant difference in your job search. A strong cover letter highlights your relevant skills, aligns with the company's needs, and demonstrates your enthusiasm for the role. By following the tips in this chapter, you can create a compelling cover letter that captures the attention of hiring managers and increases your chances of landing an interview. Remember, a great cover letter complements your resume and sets the stage for showcasing your qualifications and passion for the job.

Chapter 5: Optimizing Your LinkedIn Profile for Tech Recruiters

LinkedIn is a powerful tool for anyone looking to build a career in tech. Recruiters use LinkedIn to find candidates, and having a strong profile can help you stand out and attract job opportunities. In this chapter, we'll explore how to optimize your LinkedIn profile to catch the eye of tech recruiters and make the most of this professional network.

Crafting a Compelling Headline

Your headline is one of the first things people see when they visit your profile. It should quickly convey who you are and what you do. Instead of just listing your job title, consider highlighting your key skills or the type of roles you're interested in.

For example, instead of "Software Engineer," you could write "Software Engineer | Python Developer | AI Enthusiast." This gives a clearer picture of your expertise and interests.

Writing an Engaging Summary

The summary section is your opportunity to tell your story. It's like the cover letter of your LinkedIn profile. Start with a strong opening that grabs attention and briefly introduces who you are and what you do.

For instance, "I am a passionate software developer with over five years of experience in building scalable web applications. I specialize in Python and JavaScript and have a keen interest in artificial intelligence and machine learning. I love solving complex problems and creating innovative solutions that make a difference."

Use the rest of the summary to highlight your key achievements, skills, and what you're looking for in your next role. Keep it concise, engaging, and easy to read. Use bullet points to break up the text and make it more digestible.

Highlighting Your Experience

Your work experience section should provide a detailed look at your professional background. List your job titles, companies, and dates of employment. For each position, include a few bullet points that describe your responsibilities and accomplishments.

Focus on achievements that showcase your skills and the impact you made. Use numbers and specific examples to quantify your success whenever possible. For example, "Developed a web application that increased user engagement by 30%" is more impactful than "Developed a web application."

Showcasing Your Skills

LinkedIn allows you to list up to 50 skills on your profile. Make sure to include the most relevant skills for the tech industry and the roles you're targeting. Recruiters often search for candidates based on specific skills, so having these listed can increase your visibility.

Endorsements from colleagues and peers can also add credibility to your skills. Reach out to your network and ask for endorsements, and be sure to endorse others in return.

Adding Certifications and Courses

Certifications and courses are great ways to demonstrate your expertise and commitment to continuous learning. Include any relevant certifications, such as AWS Certified Solutions Architect, CompTIA Security+, or Certified ScrumMaster. List online courses from platforms like Coursera, Udemy, or LinkedIn Learning that are relevant to your field.

For example, "Completed a Machine Learning course on Coursera" or "Certified in Data Science by IBM." These additions show that you are proactive about keeping your skills up-to-date.

Featuring Projects and Publications

If you have worked on significant projects, whether personal or professional, include them in the "Projects" section. Describe the project, your role, the technologies used, and the outcome. Providing links to your work, such as GitHub repositories or live websites, can give recruiters a deeper insight into your abilities.

If you have written any articles, blog posts, or papers related to your field, feature them in the "Publications" section. This can showcase your expertise and thought leadership in the tech industry.

Requesting Recommendations

Recommendations from colleagues, managers, or clients can add significant value to your profile. They provide third-party validation of your skills and work ethic. Don't be shy about asking for recommendations. Reach out to people you've worked closely with and ask them to highlight specific skills or achievements.

In return, offer to write recommendations for others. This not only helps build your network but also shows your appreciation for their support.

Engaging with Content

LinkedIn is not just a static resume; it's a dynamic platform for networking and sharing knowledge. Engage with content by liking, commenting, and sharing posts related to your field. Follow industry leaders, join relevant groups, and participate in discussions.

Sharing your own content, such as articles, insights, or project updates, can position you as a thought leader and keep you visible to your network and recruiters.

Keeping Your Profile Updated
Regularly update your profile to reflect new skills, experiences, and achievements. A current profile shows that you are active and engaged in your career. Set a reminder to review and update your profile every few months.

Using Keywords Effectively
Recruiters often use keywords to search for candidates. Make sure your profile includes relevant keywords that match the jobs you're interested in. These can be specific skills, technologies, or job titles. For example, if you're

looking for a role in data science, include keywords like "data analysis," "machine learning," and "Python."

Avoid keyword stuffing, but naturally incorporate these terms throughout your profile—in your headline, summary, experience, and skills sections.

Connecting and Networking

Build your network by connecting with colleagues, classmates, and industry professionals. Personalize your connection requests with a brief message explaining why you want to connect. This can make a positive impression and increase the chances of your request being accepted.

Once connected, engage with your network by congratulating them on new roles or achievements, commenting on their posts, and sharing relevant content. Networking is about building relationships, so be genuine and supportive.

Optimizing your LinkedIn profile for tech recruiters is an ongoing process that requires attention and effort. A strong LinkedIn profile can open doors to new opportunities, showcase your skills and achievements, and help you build valuable professional relationships. By following the tips in this chapter, you can create a compelling profile that stands out to recruiters and helps you advance your career in technology and IT. Keep your profile updated, engage with your network, and stay active on the platform to maximize the benefits of LinkedIn.

Chapter 6: Networking Strategies for IT Professionals

Networking is an essential skill for IT professionals. Building connections with others in your field can lead to job opportunities, collaborations, and valuable advice. In this chapter, we will explore effective networking strategies that can help you grow your professional network and advance your career in the IT industry.

The Importance of Networking

Networking is more than just exchanging business cards or adding someone on LinkedIn. It's about building relationships and creating a support system that can help you throughout your career. Networking can lead to:

- Job opportunities: Many jobs are filled through referrals and word-of-mouth. Knowing the right people can help you get your foot in the door.
- Knowledge sharing: Networking allows you to learn from others, stay updated on industry trends, and gain new perspectives.
- Career growth: Building relationships with mentors and peers can provide guidance and support as you advance in your career.

Getting Started with Networking

If you're new to networking, it can feel intimidating. Start small and gradually build your confidence. Begin by reaching out to people you already know, such as colleagues, classmates, or friends in the industry. Let them know you're looking to expand your network and ask if they can introduce you to others.

Attending Industry Events

Industry events, such as conferences, seminars, and meetups, are great places to meet like-minded professionals. These events provide opportunities to learn about the latest trends and technologies while connecting with others who share your interests.

Before attending an event, do some research. Find out who the speakers are and which companies will be represented. This will help you identify key people you want to connect with. Prepare a few talking points or questions to initiate conversations.

During the event, be approachable and engage in conversations. Don't be afraid to introduce yourself to new people. A simple introduction like, "Hi, I'm Alex. I'm a software developer. What do you do?" can start a meaningful conversation.

Leveraging Online Platforms

Online platforms like LinkedIn, Twitter, and professional forums are powerful tools for networking. They allow you to connect with people from all over the world and participate in discussions relevant to your field.

On LinkedIn, keep your profile updated and professional. Share articles, comment on posts, and join groups related to your interests. When sending connection requests, personalize your message to explain why you want to connect.

Twitter can be a great platform for following industry leaders and participating in conversations. Share interesting content, use relevant hashtags, and engage with others by liking and retweeting their posts.

Professional forums and online communities, such as GitHub, Stack Overflow, and Reddit, offer opportunities to ask questions, share knowledge, and collaborate on projects. Actively participate in these communities to build your reputation and connect with other professionals.

Building Relationships

Building meaningful relationships takes time and effort. It's important to be genuine and show interest in others. Networking isn't just about what others can do for you, but also how you can help them.

Offer to help others by sharing your knowledge, providing feedback, or making introductions. Showing that you're willing to support others can strengthen your relationships and make people more likely to help you in return.

Keep in touch with your connections by periodically checking in, congratulating them on achievements, or sharing relevant articles. A simple message like, "Hi Sarah, I saw this article on cloud computing and thought you might find it interesting," can help maintain your relationships.

Finding Mentors and Mentees

Mentorship is a valuable aspect of networking. Having a mentor can provide guidance, support, and insights into your career. Look for mentors who have experience and knowledge in areas you want to grow in. Approach potential mentors with respect and express your interest in learning from them.

On the other hand, consider becoming a mentor to others. Sharing your knowledge and experience can be rewarding and help you build your reputation in the industry. Mentoring can also provide new perspectives and help you develop leadership skills.

Joining Professional Organizations

Professional organizations, such as the Association for Computing Machinery (ACM) or the Institute of Electrical and Electronics Engineers (IEEE), offer networking opportunities, resources, and events for IT professionals. Joining these organizations can help you connect with others in your field and stay informed about industry developments.

Many organizations have local chapters that host events and meetups. Participating in these activities can help you build relationships with professionals in your area.

Volunteering and Community Involvement

Volunteering is another effective way to network and give back to the community. Look for opportunities to volunteer at industry events, hackathons, or tech workshops. Volunteering can help you meet new people, gain new skills, and make a positive impact.

Community involvement, such as participating in local tech meetups or contributing to open-source projects, can also help you expand your network and showcase your skills. Being an active member of the community can increase your visibility and open doors to new opportunities.

Following Up

After meeting new contacts, it's important to follow up to maintain the connection. Send a brief message or email thanking them for the conversation and expressing your interest in staying in touch.

For example, "Hi John, it was great meeting you at the tech conference last week. I enjoyed our conversation about cloud computing and would love to stay in touch. Let's connect on LinkedIn."

Following up shows that you value the connection and are interested in building a relationship.

Networking is a powerful tool for IT professionals. By building relationships, attending events, leveraging online platforms, and getting involved in the community, you can expand your network and advance your career. Remember to be genuine, offer help to others, and maintain your connections over time. With these strategies, you can create a strong support system that will benefit you throughout your career in the IT industry.

Chapter 7: Mastering the Tech Job Application Process

Applying for tech jobs can feel like a daunting task, but with the right approach, you can navigate the process smoothly and increase your chances of landing your dream job. In this chapter, we'll break down each step of the job application process, offering tips and strategies to help you succeed.

Researching the Job Market
Before you start applying for jobs, it's important to understand the job market. Research the types of roles that are available, the skills that are in demand, and the companies that are hiring. Websites like LinkedIn, Glassdoor, and Indeed are great resources for this.

Make a list of companies you're interested in and follow them on social media to stay updated on their job postings and company news. Join online communities and forums related to your field to get insights and advice from other professionals.

Tailoring Your Resume and Cover Letter
Each job application should be tailored to the specific role you're applying for. Start by carefully reading the job description and highlighting the key skills and qualifications the employer is looking for.

Update your resume to emphasize your relevant experience and skills. Use keywords from the job description to make your resume more likely to pass through Applicant Tracking Systems (ATS). Focus on quantifiable achievements that demonstrate your abilities and impact.

For example, instead of saying "Worked on a team project," you could say "Led a team of 5 developers to create a web application that increased user engagement by 20%."

Your cover letter should also be tailored to each job. Use it to explain why you're interested in the role and how your skills and experience make you a good fit. Highlight specific examples from your past work that relate to the job requirements.

Applying Online

Most tech jobs are posted online, so you'll likely spend a lot of time applying through company websites and job boards. Create a system to keep track of the jobs you've applied for, including the date of application and any follow-up actions needed.

When applying online, make sure to fill out all required fields and attach your resume and cover letter. Pay attention to any additional instructions, such as providing links to your portfolio or completing an assessment.

It's also important to follow up on your applications. After submitting your application, wait a week or two and then send a polite email to the hiring manager to express your continued interest in the position and ask about the status of your application.

Networking for Job Opportunities

While applying online is important, networking can often be more effective in finding job opportunities. Many jobs are filled through referrals, so building and leveraging your professional network can give you an edge.

Let your connections know that you're looking for a job and ask if they know of any openings or can introduce you to people in your field. Attend industry events, join online communities, and participate in discussions to expand your network.

If you have contacts at a company you're interested in, reach out to them for advice or insights about the job. They may be able to refer you internally, which can increase your chances of getting an interview.

Preparing for Interviews

Once you start getting interview invitations, it's time to prepare. Research the company thoroughly, including its products, services, culture, and recent news. Review the job description again and think about how your skills and experience align with the role.

Practice common interview questions, such as "Tell me about yourself," "Why do you want to work here?" and "What are your strengths and weaknesses?" Prepare specific examples from your past work that demonstrate your skills and achievements.

For technical roles, you may also need to prepare for coding interviews or technical assessments. Practice solving coding problems on websites like LeetCode or HackerRank. Review key concepts and algorithms, and be ready to explain your thought process during the interview.

Acing the Interview

During the interview, be professional and confident. Dress appropriately, arrive on time, and bring copies of your resume and any other relevant documents. Be polite and respectful to everyone you meet, from the receptionist to the hiring manager.

When answering questions, be honest and concise. Use the STAR method (Situation, Task, Action, Result) to structure your responses and provide clear examples of your accomplishments. Show enthusiasm for the role and the company, and ask thoughtful questions that demonstrate your interest and knowledge.

For technical interviews, take your time to understand the problem and plan your approach. Communicate your thought process clearly and ask clarifying questions if needed. Even if you don't arrive at the perfect solution, showing your problem-solving skills and ability to think critically can leave a positive impression.

Following Up After the Interview

After the interview, send a thank-you email to the interviewer. Express your appreciation for the opportunity to interview and reiterate your interest in the position. Mention something specific you discussed during the interview to make your email more personal and memorable.

If you don't hear back within the expected timeframe, it's okay to send a follow-up email to ask about the status of your application. Be polite and respectful in your follow-up communication.

Negotiating Job Offers

When you receive a job offer, take the time to review it carefully. Consider the salary, benefits, work hours, company culture, and any other factors that are important to you. It's often possible to negotiate the terms of the offer, so don't be afraid to ask for what you need.

Research the average salaries for similar roles in your area to ensure the offer is competitive. Prepare a list of reasons why you're worth the salary you're requesting, such as your skills, experience, and the value you can bring to the company.

Approach the negotiation professionally and respectfully. Express your enthusiasm for the role and the company, and explain why you're asking for the specific terms. Be open to compromise and work with the employer to reach a mutually beneficial agreement.

Mastering the tech job application process takes time and effort, but with the right strategies, you can increase your chances of success. Research the job market, tailor your resume and cover letter, apply online, network for opportunities, prepare for interviews, and follow up professionally. By being proactive and persistent, you can navigate the job application process and land your dream job in the tech industry.

Chapter 8: Preparing for Technical Interviews in IT

Technical interviews can be challenging, but with the right preparation, you can approach them with confidence. These interviews are designed to test your problem-solving skills, coding abilities, and understanding of technical concepts. In this chapter, we'll cover everything you need to know to prepare effectively for technical interviews in IT.

Understanding the Technical Interview Process

The technical interview process typically consists of several stages, each designed to evaluate different aspects of your skills and experience. Common stages include:

- Phone Screen: A preliminary interview, often with a recruiter or a technical screener, to assess your basic qualifications and fit for the role.
- Coding Challenge: An online test or take-home assignment that evaluates your coding skills and problem-solving abilities.
- Technical Interview: A more in-depth interview, usually involving live coding or technical questions. This can be conducted in person or virtually.
- System Design Interview: An interview focused on your ability to design scalable and efficient systems, often for more senior positions.
- Behavioral Interview: An interview to assess your soft skills, such as communication, teamwork, and cultural fit with the company.

Knowing what to expect at each stage can help you prepare more effectively.

Reviewing Key Concepts

Technical interviews often focus on core computer science concepts. Make sure you're familiar with the following topics:

- Data Structures: Understand the basics of arrays, linked lists, stacks, queues, hash tables, trees, graphs, and heaps. Know how to implement them and their common use cases.
- Algorithms: Study sorting and searching algorithms (like quicksort, mergesort, and binary search), as well as more advanced topics like dynamic programming, recursion, and graph algorithms.
- Big O Notation: Be able to analyze the time and space complexity of algorithms.
- System Design: For system design interviews, understand how to design scalable and efficient systems. Learn about distributed systems, databases, caching, load balancing, and other key concepts.

Use resources like textbooks, online courses, and coding websites to review these topics. Practice implementing data structures and algorithms from scratch to reinforce your understanding.

Practicing Coding Problems

One of the best ways to prepare for technical interviews is to practice solving coding problems. Websites like LeetCode, HackerRank, and CodeSignal offer a wide range of problems that you can use to practice.

Start with easier problems to build your confidence and gradually move on to more challenging ones. Try to solve problems from different categories, such as arrays, strings, trees, and dynamic programming.

When practicing, focus on writing clean, efficient code. Pay attention to edge cases and think about how your solution scales with larger inputs. Time yourself to simulate the interview environment and improve your speed and accuracy.

Mock Interviews

Mock interviews are a valuable tool for preparing for technical interviews. They help you practice your problem-solving skills under pressure and get feedback on your performance.

You can do mock interviews with friends, and colleagues, or through online platforms that offer mock interview services. Choose problems that are similar in difficulty and style to what you expect in your actual interviews.

After each mock interview, review your performance. Identify areas where you struggled and work on improving them. Pay attention to the feedback you receive and use it to refine your approach.

Developing a Problem-Solving Strategy

Having a clear strategy for approaching coding problems can help you stay calm and focused during interviews. Here's a simple problem-solving strategy you can follow:

1. Understand the Problem: Read the problem statement carefully and make sure you understand the requirements. Ask clarifying questions if needed.

2. Plan Your Approach: Think about the data structures and algorithms you might use to solve the problem. Consider different approaches and choose the one that seems most efficient.

3. Write Pseudocode: Before diving into the actual code, write pseudocode to outline your approach. This helps you organize your thoughts and identify potential issues.

4. Code the Solution: Start coding your solution, following the plan you've outlined. Write clean, readable code and handle edge cases.

5. Test Your Code: Test your solution with different inputs, including edge cases, to ensure it works correctly. Debug any issues that arise.

By following this strategy, you can approach coding problems methodically and reduce the likelihood of mistakes.

Preparing for System Design Interviews

System design interviews are common for senior roles and require a different kind of preparation. These interviews test your ability to design scalable, efficient systems that can handle large amounts of data and traffic.

To prepare for system design interviews:

- Study Common Design Patterns: Learn about common design patterns used in scalable

systems, such as microservices, event-driven architecture, and load balancing.
- Understand Key Concepts: Make sure you're familiar with databases (SQL and NoSQL), caching strategies, message queues, and distributed systems.
- Practice Designing Systems: Practice designing systems for common scenarios, such as building a web crawler, a chat application, or an e-commerce platform. Think about how you would handle scalability, fault tolerance, and data consistency.

During a system design interview, clearly explain your thought process and the trade-offs you're considering. Use diagrams to illustrate your design and make your explanation easier to follow.

Behavioral Interview Preparation

While technical skills are crucial, companies also want to hire candidates who fit well with their team and culture. Behavioral interviews assess your soft skills, such as communication, teamwork, and problem-solving.

Prepare for behavioral interviews by reflecting on your past experiences. Think about specific examples that demonstrate your skills and achievements. Use the STAR method (Situation, Task, Action, Result) to structure your responses and provide clear, concise answers.

Common behavioral interview questions include:

- "Tell me about a time you faced a challenging problem at work."
- "How do you handle conflicts with teammates?"
- "Describe a project you worked on that you're particularly proud of."

Practice answering these questions out loud to build your confidence and ensure your responses are clear and well-organized.

Final Tips for Success
- Stay Calm and Confident: It's normal to feel nervous during technical interviews, but try to stay calm and focused. Remember that

interviewers are not just evaluating your technical skills but also how you approach problems and handle pressure.

- Communicate Clearly: Throughout the interview, communicate your thought process clearly. Explain your approach, ask clarifying questions, and discuss any trade-offs you're considering. Good communication can make a strong impression on interviewers.

- Learn from Each Interview: Regardless of the outcome, treat each interview as a learning experience. Reflect on what went well and what you can improve for next time. Use the feedback you receive to refine your preparation.

Preparing for technical interviews in IT requires time, effort, and a strategic approach. By understanding the interview process, reviewing key concepts, practicing coding problems, and honing your problem-solving strategy, you can increase your chances of success. Remember to prepare for system design and behavioral interviews as well, and use each interview experience as an opportunity to learn and grow.

With dedication and persistence, you can master the technical interview process and land your dream job in the IT industry.

Chapter 9: Common Tech and IT Interview Questions and How to Answer Them

Preparing for tech and IT interviews can be stressful, but knowing the types of questions you might face and how to answer them can make a big difference. In this chapter, we'll go over some common interview questions and provide tips on how to respond effectively. By practicing these questions and answers, you'll be better prepared to showcase your skills and impress your interviewers.

Tell Me About Yourself
This is often the first question in an interview and sets the tone for the rest of the conversation. It's your chance to give a brief overview of your background, experience, and why you're a good

fit for the role. Keep your answer concise and relevant to the job you're applying for.

Example Answer:
"I have a degree in Computer Science and over five years of experience as a software developer. I started my career at a small startup where I gained hands-on experience in full-stack development. Currently, I work at XYZ Company, where I've led several projects to develop web applications that improved user engagement by 30%. I'm passionate about coding and problem-solving, and I'm excited about the opportunity to bring my skills to your team."

Why Do You Want to Work Here?
This question assesses your interest in the company and whether you've done your homework. Show that you've researched the company and explain why you're excited about the role and how you can contribute.

Example Answer:

"I'm impressed by your company's commitment to innovation and your recent projects in cloud computing. I admire your focus on creating solutions that make a difference in people's lives. With my background in developing scalable cloud applications, I believe I can contribute to your team's success and help drive your projects forward."

What Are Your Strengths and Weaknesses?
This question evaluates your self-awareness and honesty. Highlight a few strengths that are relevant to the job and provide examples. For weaknesses, mention something you've worked to improve and how you've addressed it.

Example Answer:
"One of my strengths is my ability to learn new technologies quickly. For example, when our team decided to switch to a new programming language, I took the initiative to master it and help my colleagues transition smoothly. As for weaknesses, I used to struggle with public speaking. To overcome this, I joined a local

Toastmasters club and practiced regularly. Now, I feel much more confident presenting my ideas to a group."

Describe a Challenging Project You've Worked On

This question helps interviewers understand how you handle difficulties and solve problems. Choose a specific project, and explain the challenges you faced, and how you overcame them.

Example Answer:
"One challenging project I worked on was developing a real-time data processing system for a financial services client. The main challenge was ensuring the system could handle high volumes of data with low latency. I worked closely with my team to optimize our algorithms and implemented efficient data structures to improve performance. After several iterations and testing, we successfully delivered a system that met the client's requirements and handled data processing in under a second."

How Do You Handle Tight Deadlines?

Employers want to know if you can work under pressure and manage your time effectively. Provide an example of a time when you met a tight deadline and describe the steps you took to achieve it.

Example Answer:

"In my previous job, we had a major product release that required all features to be completed and tested within a month. To meet the deadline, I prioritized my tasks, broke them down into manageable parts, and set daily goals. I also communicated regularly with my team to ensure we were all on track. By staying organized and focused, we managed to complete the project on time and with high quality."

Can You Explain [Technical Concept]?

Interviewers often ask technical questions to assess your knowledge and ability to explain complex concepts clearly. Be prepared to explain fundamental concepts related to your field, such as data structures, algorithms, or networking.

Example Answer:
"Sure, let's talk about binary search. Binary search is an efficient algorithm for finding an item in a sorted list. It works by repeatedly dividing the search interval in half. If the item is less than the middle element, the search continues in the lower half; if it's greater, the search continues in the upper half. This process repeats until the item is found or the interval is empty. Binary search has a time complexity of $O(\log n)$, making it much faster than linear search for large datasets."

How Do You Stay Updated with New Technologies?

The tech industry is constantly evolving, and employers want to know that you stay current with new developments. Describe the methods you use to keep your skills and knowledge up to date.

Example Answer:
"I stay updated with new technologies by regularly reading tech blogs, following industry leaders on social media, and participating in online courses. I also attend local meetups and conferences to network with other professionals and learn about the latest trends. Recently, I completed a course on machine learning, which has given me new insights into how to apply these techniques to real-world problems."

Describe a Time When You Had to Work with a Difficult Team Member
This question assesses your interpersonal skills and ability to handle conflicts. Choose a specific example, explain the situation, and how you resolved it constructively.

Example Answer:
"In one project, I had a team member who frequently missed deadlines, which affected our progress. I decided to address the issue directly by having a one-on-one conversation with them. I listened to their concerns and found out they

were struggling with some aspects of the project. We agreed on a plan to provide them with additional support and set more realistic deadlines. By improving communication and offering help, we were able to get back on track and complete the project successfully."

What Are Your Career Goals?

Employers want to know if your long-term goals align with the company's objectives. Describe your career aspirations and how the position you're applying for fits into your plans.

Example Answer:

"My career goal is to become an expert in cybersecurity. I'm passionate about protecting systems and data from threats, and I've been continuously learning and gaining certifications in this field. This position aligns with my goals because it offers opportunities to work on challenging security projects and further develop my skills. I'm excited about the chance to grow with your company and contribute to its success in the cybersecurity space."

How Do You Approach Learning a New Technology?

Tech roles often require you to learn new tools and technologies quickly. Explain your process for learning and adapting to new technologies.

Example Answer:
"When I need to learn a new technology, I start by researching its fundamentals through documentation, tutorials, and online courses. I also like to work on small projects to apply what I've learned and gain practical experience. For instance, when I had to learn Docker for a recent project, I took an online course, read the official documentation, and built a few containerized applications to get hands-on practice. This approach helps me understand the technology deeply and apply it effectively in my work."

Preparing for common tech and IT interview questions can significantly boost your confidence and performance. By understanding what interviewers are looking for and practicing your answers, you can showcase your skills and experiences effectively. Remember to tailor your responses to each specific role and company, and always provide concrete examples to back up your claims. With thorough preparation and a positive attitude, you can excel in your tech and IT interviews and move closer to landing your dream job.

Chapter 10: Technical Skills Assessment and Coding Tests

When applying for tech and IT jobs, you'll likely face technical skills assessments and coding tests. These evaluations are crucial because they show employers your ability to solve problems, write clean code, and think logically. Preparing for these tests can be challenging, but with the right approach, you can excel.

Understanding Coding Tests
Coding tests are designed to measure your programming skills and problem-solving abilities. They can take various forms, such as online tests, take-home assignments, or live coding sessions. Employers use these tests to see how you approach problems, how well you understand algorithms and data structures, and how efficiently you can write code.

Online coding tests are often the first step in the interview process. These tests are usually time-limited and administered through platforms like HackerRank, LeetCode, or CodeSignal. They include a range of problems from basic to advanced levels. Take-home assignments give you more time to work on a problem, allowing you to showcase your coding style and attention to detail. Live coding sessions involve solving problems in real time, often with an interviewer watching and asking questions.

Preparing for Coding Tests

Preparation is key to performing well on coding tests. Here are some steps you can take to get ready:

1. Master the Basics: Start by reviewing the basics of the programming language you'll be using. Make sure you're comfortable with syntax, common functions, and data structures like arrays, linked lists, stacks, queues, hash tables, trees, and graphs.

2. Study Algorithms: Understand the most common algorithms, such as sorting (quick sort, merge sort), searching (binary search), and dynamic programming. Learn how to implement these algorithms and analyze their time and space complexity using Big O notation.

3. Practice, Practice, Practice: Use online platforms like LeetCode, HackerRank, and CodeSignal to practice coding problems. Start with easy problems to build your confidence and gradually move on to more difficult ones. Aim to solve a variety of problems, including arrays, strings, linked lists, trees, graphs, and dynamic programming.

4. Simulate Test Conditions: When practicing, try to simulate test conditions by timing yourself and working in a quiet environment. This helps you get used to the pressure of a real coding test.

5. Learn to Debug: Debugging is an essential skill. Practice finding and fixing errors in your code. Use print statements and debugging tools

to understand what's going wrong and how to correct it.

6. Review Past Mistakes: Keep track of the problems you find difficult or get wrong. Review them regularly to understand your mistakes and learn from them.

Approaching Coding Problems
Having a strategy for solving coding problems can make a big difference. Here's a step-by-step approach to help you tackle coding challenges effectively:

1. Read the Problem Carefully: Start by reading the problem statement thoroughly. Make sure you understand the requirements and constraints. Clarify any doubts you have before you start coding.

2. Plan Your Solution: Before writing any code, plan your approach. Think about which data structures and algorithms are best suited for the

problem. Consider different approaches and choose the most efficient one.

3. Write Pseudocode: Outline your solution in pseudocode. This helps you organize your thoughts and ensures you have a clear plan before diving into the actual code.

4. Code Your Solution: Start coding your solution based on your plan. Write clean, readable code and follow best practices. Use meaningful variable names and add comments where necessary.

5. Test Your Code: Test your code with various inputs, including edge cases, to ensure it works correctly. Look out for any bugs or performance issues and address them.

6. Optimize if Needed: If you have time, review your solution and look for ways to optimize it. Consider improving the time and space complexity if possible.

Handling Live Coding Interviews

Live coding interviews can be nerve-wracking, but they also provide a chance to demonstrate your thought process and communication skills. Here are some tips to succeed in live coding sessions:

1. Communicate Clearly: Explain your thought process as you solve the problem. Let the interviewer know what you're thinking, why you're choosing a particular approach, and how you plan to implement it. This shows that you can think logically and articulate your ideas clearly.

2. Ask Questions: If you're unsure about any part of the problem, don't hesitate to ask questions. Clarifying doubts early can save you from making mistakes later on.

3. Stay Calm: It's normal to feel nervous but try to stay calm and focused. If you get stuck, take a deep breath and review the problem statement.

Sometimes, a short pause can help you see the solution more clearly.

4. Think Aloud: Verbalizing your thoughts can help you stay focused and make it easier for the interviewer to follow your logic. It also demonstrates your problem-solving process.

5. Write Readable Code: Even under time pressure, aim to write clean and readable code. Use consistent formatting, and meaningful variable names, and add comments where necessary.

6. Handle Mistakes Gracefully: If you make a mistake, don't panic. Acknowledge it, explain what went wrong, and how you plan to fix it. This shows resilience and problem-solving skills.

Tackling Take-Home Assignments

Take-home assignments allow you to demonstrate your coding skills in a less pressured environment. However, they also require thoroughness and attention to detail. Here's how to approach take-home assignments effectively:

1. Understand the Requirements: Carefully read the instructions and understand what's expected. Make sure you know the deliverables and any constraints.

2. Plan Your Work: Break down the assignment into smaller tasks and create a plan. Allocate time for each task and stick to your schedule.

3. Write Clean Code: Take the time to write clean, well-documented code. Follow best practices for coding standards and use comments to explain your logic.

4. Test Thoroughly: Test your code with various inputs to ensure it works correctly. Pay attention to edge cases and potential issues.

5. Review and Refine: Before submitting, review your work thoroughly. Look for any mistakes,

optimize your code if necessary, and ensure your solution meets all the requirements.

Technical skills assessments and coding tests are a vital part of the hiring process for tech and IT jobs. By understanding the types of tests you might face, preparing thoroughly, and following a structured approach to solving problems, you can perform confidently and showcase your abilities effectively. Whether you're tackling online tests, live coding sessions, or take-home assignments, practice and preparation are key to success. With dedication and effort, you can master these challenges and move closer to securing your dream job in the tech industry.

Chapter 11: Showcasing Your Tech Projects and Portfolio

Creating a strong portfolio is one of the best ways to stand out to potential employers in the tech and IT industry. A well-organized portfolio highlights your skills, experience, and the projects you've worked on, giving recruiters a clear picture of what you can do. In this chapter, we'll discuss how to build a compelling portfolio and showcase your tech projects effectively.

Why a Portfolio Matters
In the competitive tech job market, a resume alone might not be enough to catch an employer's attention. A portfolio allows you to provide concrete evidence of your skills and experience. It demonstrates your ability to complete projects, solve problems, and apply your knowledge in real-world scenarios.

Choosing Projects to Showcase

Start by selecting the best projects to include in your portfolio. Choose projects that:

1. Highlight Your Skills: Pick projects that demonstrate your strongest skills, whether it's coding, design, problem-solving, or something else.
2. Show Variety: Include a range of projects that showcase different skills and technologies. This shows your versatility and ability to learn new things.
3. Have a Clear Impact: Select projects that have had a significant impact, whether it's solving a major problem, improving performance, or creating something new.

Describing Your Projects

For each project in your portfolio, provide a detailed description. Include the following elements:

1. Title and Description: Give your project a clear title and write a brief overview of what it is and what it does.

2. Your Role: Describe your role in the project. Did you work on it alone or as part of a team? What were your specific responsibilities?

3. Technologies Used: List the technologies, tools, and languages you used to complete the project.

4. Challenges and Solutions: Explain any challenges you faced and how you overcame them. This shows your problem-solving skills.

5. Outcome and Impact: Describe the results of the project. Did it improve performance, save time, or solve a specific problem? Include any metrics or data that demonstrate its success.

6. Code Samples and Screenshots: If possible, include code snippets and screenshots. This

gives recruiters a visual understanding of your work.

Organizing Your Portfolio

Your portfolio should be well-organized and easy to navigate. Here are some tips:

1. Use a Clean Layout: Choose a clean, professional layout that makes it easy to find information. Avoid clutter and keep the design simple.

2. Create Sections: Divide your portfolio into sections for different types of projects, such as web development, mobile apps, data science, etc.

3. Include a Summary: Start with a summary section that provides an overview of your skills and experience. This helps recruiters get a quick sense of who you are and what you can do.

4. Provide Contact Information: Make sure to include your contact information so recruiters can easily reach out to you.

Using GitHub for Your Portfolio
GitHub is a popular platform for showcasing coding projects. It allows you to host your code repositories and share them with potential employers. Here's how to make the most of GitHub:

1. Create a Professional Profile: Set up a professional GitHub profile with a clear photo, bio, and links to your other profiles or website.

2. Organize Your Repositories: Keep your repositories well-organized and properly named. Use README files to provide an overview of each project.

3. Highlight Key Projects: Pin your most important projects to the top of your GitHub profile so they're easy to find.

4. Maintain a Clean Code: Ensure your code is clean, well-documented, and follows best practices. This demonstrates your attention to detail and professionalism.

5. Use GitHub Pages: You can use GitHub Pages to create a personal website for your portfolio. This allows you to showcase your projects in a more visually appealing way.

Building a Personal Website
Creating a personal website is a great way to showcase your portfolio in a customized and professional manner. Here's how to build an effective personal website:

1. Choose a Domain Name: Select a domain name that includes your name or a variation of it. This makes it easy for recruiters to find you online.

2. Use a Website Builder: If you're not experienced in web development, use a website

builder like Wix, Squarespace, or WordPress to create your site. These platforms offer templates that you can customize.

3. Design for Clarity: Keep the design simple and professional. Use a clean layout, easy-to-read fonts, and a consistent color scheme.

4. Include Key Sections: Your website should have sections for your resume, portfolio, about me, and contact information. Include links to your GitHub, LinkedIn, and other relevant profiles.

5. Showcase Your Best Work: Highlight your most impressive projects on the homepage or in a dedicated portfolio section. Use images, videos, and descriptions to provide a clear understanding of your work.

6. Keep It Updated: Regularly update your website with new projects, skills, and achievements. An up-to-date portfolio shows that you're actively engaged in your field.

Making Your Portfolio Stand Out

To make your portfolio stand out, focus on what makes you unique. Here are some tips:

1. Tell Your Story: Share your personal journey, including how you got into tech, what motivates you, and your career goals. This helps employers connect with you on a personal level.

2. Highlight Achievements: Include any awards, certifications, or recognitions you've received. These add credibility to your portfolio.

3. Show Your Process: Document your process for each project. Explain how you approached the problem, the steps you took, and the reasoning behind your decisions. This provides insight into your thought process and problem-solving skills.

4. Include Testimonials: If possible, include testimonials from colleagues, professors, or

clients. Positive feedback from others can boost your credibility.

5. Add a Blog: Consider adding a blog to your website where you write about your experiences, projects, and thoughts on industry trends. This shows your engagement with the tech community and your commitment to continuous learning.

A strong portfolio is essential for showcasing your skills and experience to potential employers. By carefully selecting and describing your projects, organizing your portfolio effectively, and using platforms like GitHub and personal websites, you can create a compelling presentation of your work. Remember to keep your portfolio updated and make it unique to stand out from the competition. With a well-crafted portfolio, you can demonstrate your capabilities and move closer to landing your dream job in tech and IT.

Chapter 12: Leveraging Certifications in the Tech Industry

Certifications can play a crucial role in your tech career. They validate your skills, show your commitment to learning, and can make you stand out to employers. This chapter will explore how to choose the right certifications, prepare for them, and use them to boost your career in the tech industry.

The Importance of Certifications
In the fast-paced world of technology, staying updated with the latest skills and knowledge is essential. Certifications help you do just that. They are official recognitions from respected organizations that prove you have specific skills and knowledge. For employers, certifications are a quick way to gauge your expertise and dedication to your field. They can be particularly

important if you're looking to switch careers, seek promotions, or enter competitive job markets.

Choosing the Right Certifications

With so many certifications available, it can be challenging to know which ones to pursue. Here are some factors to consider when choosing certifications:

1. Relevance to Your Career Goals: Think about what you want to achieve in your career. If you're aiming for a role in network security, for instance, a certification like CompTIA Security+ or Certified Information Systems Security Professional (CISSP) would be relevant.

2. Industry Recognition: Choose certifications that are well-recognized and respected in the industry. Employers are more likely to value certifications from reputable organizations like Microsoft, Cisco, AWS, and Google.

3. Job Market Demand: Research the job market to see which certifications are in demand. Look at job postings for your desired role and see what certifications employers are looking for.

4. Your Current Skills and Experience: Consider your current level of knowledge and experience. Some certifications require a certain level of experience before you can take the exam. Choose certifications that match your skill level and build on what you already know.

Popular Certifications in the Tech Industry
Here are some widely recognized certifications across different tech domains:

1. CompTIA A+: A good starting point for those new to IT, covering foundational IT skills and knowledge.

2. Cisco Certified Network Associate (CCNA): Ideal for networking professionals, covering networking fundamentals, IP services, security fundamentals, and more.

3. AWS Certified Solutions Architect – Associate: Great for cloud professionals, focusing on designing and deploying scalable systems on AWS.

4. Certified Information Systems Security Professional (CISSP): Highly respected in the field of cybersecurity, covering a wide range of security topics.

5. Microsoft Certified: Azure Solutions Architect Expert: For those specializing in Microsoft Azure, covering skills needed to design cloud and hybrid solutions.

6. Certified ScrumMaster (CSM): For professionals in project management, particularly in Agile environments, focusing on Scrum principles and practices.

Preparing for Certification Exams

Once you've chosen a certification, the next step is to prepare for the exam. Here are some tips to help you succeed:

1. Understand the Exam Format: Familiarize yourself with the exam format, including the types of questions and the topics covered. Most certification bodies provide detailed exam blueprints that outline what you need to study.

2. Study Materials: Gather study materials such as books, online courses, practice exams, and official study guides. Many organizations offer their own study resources, which can be very helpful.

3. Create a Study Plan: Set a study schedule that allows you to cover all the necessary topics before the exam date. Break down the material into manageable sections and stick to your plan.

4. Hands-On Practice: Practical experience is crucial. Set up a lab environment where you can practice the skills you're learning. This could be

a virtual lab or physical hardware, depending on the certification.

5. Join Study Groups: Join online forums or study groups where you can discuss topics with others who are preparing for the same exam. This can provide valuable insights and support.

6. Take Practice Exams: Practice exams help you get used to the format and timing of the real exam. They also identify areas where you need more study.

7. Stay Consistent: Regular, consistent study is more effective than cramming at the last minute. Make studying a part of your daily routine.

Taking the Certification Exam
On the day of the exam, it's important to be well-prepared and stay calm. Here are some tips to help you perform your best:

1. Get Plenty of Rest: Ensure you get a good night's sleep before the exam day. Being well-rested will help you think more clearly.

2. Arrive Early: Arrive at the testing center early to give yourself plenty of time to check in and relax before the exam starts.

3. Bring Necessary Materials: Bring any required identification and materials, such as a calculator or scratch paper, if allowed.

4. Read Questions Carefully: Take your time to read each question carefully before answering. Pay attention to details and avoid rushing.

5. Manage Your Time: Keep an eye on the time and pace yourself. If you get stuck on a question, move on and come back to it later if you have time.

6. Stay Calm: If you feel anxious, take a few deep breaths to calm yourself. Remember, you've prepared for this.

Leveraging Your Certification

After passing your certification exam, it's time to showcase your new credentials. Here's how to make the most of your certification:

1. Update Your Resume and LinkedIn Profile: Add your new certification to your resume and LinkedIn profile. Highlight it prominently so employers can easily see it.

2. Share Your Achievement: Share your success on social media platforms and professional networks. This not only celebrates your achievement but also shows potential employers your commitment to professional development.

3. Apply for Jobs: Start applying for jobs that require or prefer the certification you've earned. Use your certification as a key selling point in your applications and interviews.

4. Network: Attend industry events, conferences, and meetups to network with other

professionals. Your certification can be a great conversation starter and help you make valuable connections.

5. Seek Promotions: If you're currently employed, let your employer know about your new certification. It can be a powerful argument for a promotion or raise.

6. Continue Learning: Certifications often need to be renewed periodically. Stay updated with industry trends and continue learning to keep your skills relevant.

Certifications are a powerful tool in the tech industry. They validate your skills, open up new career opportunities, and show your dedication to professional growth. By choosing the right certifications, preparing thoroughly, and leveraging them effectively, you can significantly boost your career. Whether you're starting in tech or looking to advance your career, certifications can help you achieve your goals and stand out in the competitive job market.

Chapter 13: Understanding Different Tech Job Roles and Their Requirements

The tech industry offers a wide range of job roles, each with its unique requirements and responsibilities. Understanding these roles can help you find the best fit for your skills and interests. In this chapter, we'll explore some of the most common tech job roles and what you need to succeed in them.

Software Developer
Software developers create applications and systems that run on computers and other devices. They write, test, and maintain code to ensure software functions correctly. There are various specializations within software development,

such as front-end, back-end, and full-stack development.

- Front-End Developer: Focuses on the user interface (UI) and experience (UX). They work with HTML, CSS, and JavaScript to create visually appealing and user-friendly websites.
- Back-End Developer: Handles the server side of applications, working with databases, servers, and APIs. They use languages like Java, Python, Ruby, and Node.js.
- Full-Stack Developer: Combines front-end and back-end skills, capable of working on both the UI and server-side components of an application.

To become a software developer, you need strong programming skills, problem-solving abilities, and a solid understanding of software development principles. A degree in computer science can be helpful, but many developers also succeed through self-learning and coding boot camps.

Data Scientist

Data scientists analyze and interpret complex data to help organizations make informed decisions. They use statistical methods, machine learning, and data visualization tools to uncover trends and patterns.

Key skills for data scientists include proficiency in programming languages like Python and R, knowledge of statistical analysis, and experience with data visualization tools like Tableau and Power BI. A background in mathematics, statistics, or computer science is often required.

Network Engineer

Network engineers design, implement, and manage computer networks to ensure reliable and efficient communication between devices. They work with hardware like routers, switches, and firewalls, and use protocols to configure and troubleshoot networks.

To excel as a network engineer, you need a deep understanding of networking concepts, experience with network hardware, and knowledge of protocols like TCP/IP.

Certifications such as Cisco's CCNA or CompTIA Network+ can boost your credentials.

Cybersecurity Specialist
Cybersecurity specialists protect an organization's systems and data from cyber threats. They monitor networks for security breaches, implement security measures, and respond to incidents.

Key skills for cybersecurity specialists include knowledge of security protocols, experience with security tools and technologies, and the ability to identify and mitigate threats. Certifications like CompTIA Security+, CISSP, and Certified Ethical Hacker (CEH) are valuable in this field.

Cloud Engineer
Cloud engineers manage an organization's cloud computing infrastructure. They design, deploy, and maintain cloud-based systems and services.

To become a cloud engineer, you need knowledge of cloud platforms like AWS, Azure, or Google Cloud, experience with cloud-based applications, and an understanding of networking and security in the cloud. Certifications such as AWS Certified Solutions Architect and Microsoft Certified: Azure Solutions Architect Expert are beneficial.

IT Support Specialist

IT support specialists help users troubleshoot and resolve technical issues with their hardware, software, and network. They provide assistance via phone, email, or in person and ensure that IT systems run smoothly.

Key skills for IT support specialists include strong problem-solving abilities, excellent communication skills, and a good understanding of various operating systems and software applications. A degree in information technology or a related field can be helpful, as well as certifications like CompTIA A+.

DevOps Engineer

DevOps engineers bridge the gap between development and operations teams to improve the software development lifecycle. They automate processes, manage infrastructure, and ensure continuous integration and delivery.

To excel as a DevOps engineer, you need skills in scripting and automation, experience with tools like Jenkins, Docker, and Kubernetes, and knowledge of cloud platforms. A background in software development or IT operations is often required.

UX/UI Designer

UX/UI designers focus on creating user-friendly interfaces and enhancing user experience. They conduct user research, design wireframes and prototypes, and collaborate with developers to implement designs.

Key skills for UX/UI designers include proficiency in design tools like Sketch, Figma, and Adobe XD, a strong understanding of user-centered design principles, and the ability to create visually appealing and functional designs. A degree in design or a related field can be helpful.

Database Administrator

Database administrators manage and maintain an organization's databases, ensuring data is stored securely and efficiently. They handle tasks like database design, performance tuning, and backup and recovery.

To become a database administrator, you need knowledge of database management systems (DBMS) like SQL Server, Oracle, or MySQL, experience with database programming, and strong problem-solving skills. Certifications like Oracle Certified Professional or Microsoft Certified: Azure Database Administrator Associate can boost your credentials.

Systems Analyst

Systems analysts evaluate an organization's IT systems and processes to recommend improvements and solutions. They gather requirements, analyze data, and work with stakeholders to design and implement new systems.

Key skills for systems analysts include strong analytical abilities, knowledge of business processes, and experience with system design and implementation. A degree in computer science, information systems, or a related field is often required.

Project Manager

Project managers oversee the planning, execution, and completion of IT projects. They coordinate teams, manage budgets and timelines, and ensure projects meet their goals and objectives.

To excel as a project manager, you need strong organizational and leadership skills, the ability to manage multiple tasks, and experience with project management methodologies like Agile or Scrum. Certifications like Project Management Professional (PMP) or Certified ScrumMaster (CSM) can be valuable.

The tech industry offers a diverse range of job roles, each with its unique requirements and responsibilities. Whether you're interested in coding, data analysis, networking, cybersecurity, cloud computing, or design, there's a role that fits your skills and interests. By understanding the different tech job roles and what they entail,

you can make informed decisions about your career path and take the necessary steps to succeed. Keep learning,
stay updated with industry trends, and continue building your skills to thrive in the dynamic and ever-evolving world of technology.

Chapter 14: Salary Negotiation Tips for IT Professionals

Negotiating your salary can be one of the most challenging and crucial aspects of your career. Getting the right compensation not only affects your financial well-being but also impacts your job satisfaction and future growth. This chapter will guide you through effective strategies for negotiating your salary as an IT professional, helping you secure a compensation package that reflects your skills and experience.

Understanding Your Worth
Before entering into salary negotiations, it's essential to understand your value in the job market. Research industry standards and salary ranges for your role by looking at job boards, salary surveys, and industry reports. Websites like Glassdoor, LinkedIn Salary, and Payscale

can provide valuable insights into what similar roles are paying in your area.

Consider factors such as your experience, skills, and education. If you have specialized skills or certifications that are in high demand, you may be able to command a higher salary. Also, take into account the cost of living in your area and how it might affect your salary expectations.

Preparing for the Negotiation

Preparation is key to successful salary negotiation. Here's how to get ready:

1. Know Your Market Value: Gather information about the average salary for your position and location. This will give you a realistic idea of what you can expect and help you make a strong case during negotiations.

2. List Your Achievements: Make a list of your accomplishments, skills, and any certifications that add value to your role. Be ready to discuss how your work has positively impacted your previous employers or current job.

3. Understand the Employer's Position: Research the company's financial health and compensation practices. Knowing if they're in a growth phase or facing budget constraints can help you tailor your negotiation approach.

4. Practice Your Pitch: Rehearse how you'll present your case for a higher salary. Focus on your strengths, achievements, and market research. Practicing will make you more confident and articulate during the actual negotiation.

During the Negotiation
When you're at the negotiation table, it's important to approach the conversation with a positive and professional attitude. Here's how to handle it effectively:

1. Start with a Positive Note: Begin the conversation by expressing your enthusiasm for the role and the company. Highlight your

interest in contributing to their success and your excitement about the opportunity.

2. Present Your Case Clearly: Share your research and achievements, and explain why you believe a higher salary is justified. Be specific about your skills, experience, and any unique contributions you bring to the table.

3. Be Ready to Discuss Benefits: Sometimes employers may be unable to meet your salary request but can offer other benefits such as additional vacation days, flexible working hours, or professional development opportunities. Be open to discussing these options if the salary is not negotiable.

4. Stay Professional: Keep the conversation focused on your qualifications and the value you bring. Avoid discussing personal financial needs or comparing your offer with those of other candidates.

5. Be Prepared to Negotiate: Be ready to handle counter offers or compromise. If the employer offers a lower salary than you expected, consider negotiating for other perks or benefits that could enhance your overall compensation package.

6. Avoid Making Quick Decisions: Take your time to consider any offers or counteroffers. If needed, request a day or two to review the terms and make an informed decision.

After the Negotiation

Once the negotiation is complete, there are a few final steps to ensure everything is handled smoothly:

1. Get Everything in Writing: Once you've agreed to the terms, request a written offer that outlines the salary and any other negotiated benefits. This helps avoid any misunderstandings later on.

2. Review the Offer Carefully: Examine the written offer to ensure all agreed-upon terms are

accurately reflected. Check for any discrepancies or missing details.

3. Express Gratitude: Regardless of the outcome, thank the employer for their time and consideration. Showing appreciation can leave a positive impression and set the tone for your future relationship with the company.

4. Prepare for the New Role: Once you've accepted the offer, start preparing for your new role. Familiarize yourself with the company's culture and goals to ensure a smooth transition.

Handling Rejection or Low Offers
If the employer is unable to meet your salary expectations or if the offer is lower than anticipated, you have a few options:

1. Evaluate the Entire Package: Assess the complete compensation package, including benefits, work-life balance, and growth opportunities. Sometimes a lower salary may be offset by other valuable aspects of the job.

2. Negotiate Other Aspects: If the salary isn't flexible, consider negotiating other aspects such as additional vacation time, a signing bonus, or a performance review after a certain period with the potential for a salary increase.

3. Decide If It's Worth It: Decide whether the offer aligns with your career goals and financial needs. If it doesn't, you may choose to continue your job search.

4. Keep the Door Open: Even if you decline the offer, maintain a positive relationship with the employer. You never know when another opportunity might arise with the same company.

Salary negotiation is a critical skill that can significantly impact your career and financial future. By understanding your worth, preparing thoroughly, and approaching the negotiation with confidence and professionalism, you can improve your chances of securing a compensation package that meets your needs and reflects your value. Remember, negotiation is not just about getting a higher salary but also about finding a mutually beneficial agreement that supports your career growth and job satisfaction.

Chapter 15: Working with Tech Recruiters and Staffing Agencies

Navigating the job market can be challenging, but working with tech recruiters and staffing agencies can offer valuable support and open doors to new opportunities. These professionals specialize in connecting job seekers with employers and can be instrumental in helping you find the right tech role. This chapter will guide you through the process of working effectively with tech recruiters and staffing agencies, helping you make the most of these resources.

Understanding the Role of Tech Recruiters
Tech recruiters are professionals who specialize in finding and placing candidates in technology-related roles. They work for recruitment agencies or as independent consultants and have

deep knowledge of the tech industry and its job market.

Recruiters play a key role in matching candidates with job openings. They often have established relationships with hiring managers and companies, giving them access to job opportunities that might not be advertised publicly. They can provide insights into the hiring process, company culture, and the specific requirements of different roles.

Finding the Right Recruiter or Agency

To work effectively with a recruiter or staffing agency, it's important to choose one that aligns with your career goals and industry. Here's how to find the right match:

1. Research Agencies: Look for staffing agencies and recruiters that specialize in technology and IT roles. Check their websites, read reviews, and see if they have experience placing candidates in roles similar to what you're seeking.

2. Check Their Track Record: Look into the agency's history and success rate in placing candidates. A reputable agency will have a proven track record of successfully matching candidates with tech positions.

3. Network for Recommendations: Ask for recommendations from colleagues, mentors, or industry contacts. Personal referrals can lead you to trusted recruiters and agencies with a good reputation.

4. Evaluate Their Expertise: Ensure that the recruiter or agency has a strong understanding of the tech industry and the specific roles you're interested in. They should be familiar with the skills, technologies, and job market trends relevant to your career.

Preparing to Work with Recruiters
Once you've selected a recruiter or staffing agency, it's time to prepare for a productive partnership. Here's how to get ready:

1. Update Your Resume and LinkedIn Profile: Ensure your resume and LinkedIn profile are current and accurately reflect your skills, experience, and career goals. Recruiters will use these documents to match you with potential job opportunities.

2. Define Your Career Goals: Clearly articulate your career goals, preferred job roles, and any specific companies or industries you're interested in. This will help the recruiter understand what you're looking for and find suitable opportunities.

3. Be Honest About Your Preferences: Share your salary expectations, preferred work location, and any other job preferences with your recruiter. Being upfront about your needs will help them find opportunities that align with your expectations.

4. Prepare for Interviews: Be ready for initial discussions and interviews with the recruiter. They may ask you questions about your skills,

experience, and job preferences. Practice your responses and be prepared to discuss your career goals in detail.

Working with Recruiters During the Job Search
Once you start working with a recruiter, there are several ways to ensure the process goes smoothly:

1. Communicate Regularly: Keep in touch with your recruiter and provide updates on your job search. If your job preferences or availability change, let them know promptly.

2. Be Responsive: Respond quickly to communications from your recruiter. Timely responses can help you stay at the top of their list and increase your chances of being considered for opportunities.

3. Provide Feedback: After interviews or discussions with potential employers, share your feedback with your recruiter. This helps them

understand your impressions and adjust their search if needed.

4. Trust Their Expertise: Recruiters have valuable insights into the job market and hiring process. Trust their advice and be open to their suggestions, whether it's about negotiating offers or improving your resume.

5. Stay Positive: Job searching can be stressful, but maintaining a positive attitude can make the process smoother. A positive attitude can also leave a good impression on recruiters and potential employers.

Understanding the Recruiter's Role in the Hiring Process

Tech recruiters are your advocates in the hiring process, but they also have responsibilities to the employers they work with. Here's what you need to know:

1. Matching Candidates with Jobs: Recruiters work to match candidates with job openings that

align with their skills and career goals. They aim to find the best fit for both the candidate and the employer.

2. **Preparing Candidates for Interviews:** Recruiters often provide guidance on preparing for interviews, including tips on what to expect and how to present yourself effectively.

3. **Negotiating Offers:** Recruiters can assist with negotiating job offers, including salary, benefits, and other terms. They act as intermediaries between you and the employer to ensure a fair agreement.

4. **Providing Feedback:** Recruiters provide feedback from employers and help you understand how you can improve your candidacy. This feedback can be valuable for future job searches.

Navigating Potential Challenges

While working with recruiters can be beneficial, there can also be challenges. Here's how to navigate them:

1. Limited Job Opportunities: Sometimes, recruiters may have limited opportunities that match your specific criteria. If this happens, continue your job search independently while maintaining a relationship with the recruiter.

2. Communication Gaps: Occasionally, there may be delays or gaps in communication. If you're not receiving updates, reach out to the recruiter to check on the status of your search.

3. Unmet Expectations: If a recruiter's suggested opportunities don't align with your goals, communicate your concerns and preferences clearly. A good recruiter will adjust their search based on your feedback.

4. Exclusivity Agreements: Some recruiters may ask for exclusivity, meaning they're the only ones helping you with your job search. If you're

uncomfortable with this, discuss it openly and consider finding a recruiter who offers more flexibility.

Leveraging Staffing Agencies for Temporary or Contract Work

In addition to permanent positions, staffing agencies can help you find temporary or contract work. This can be a great option if you're looking to gain experience, explore different roles, or bridge the gap between permanent positions. Here's how to make the most of temporary or contract work through staffing agencies:

1. Be Open to Various Opportunities: Temporary or contract roles can lead to permanent positions or valuable networking connections. Be open to different types of work and experiences.

2. Understand the Terms: Ensure you're clear on the terms of temporary or contract positions,

including duration, pay rates, and any benefits or perks.

3. Use the Experience Wisely: Treat temporary or contract roles as a chance to build your skills, expand your network, and gain insights into different companies and industries.

Working with tech recruiters and staffing agencies can be a valuable part of your job search strategy. By understanding their role, preparing effectively, and maintaining clear communication, you can enhance your chances of finding the right tech role. Whether you're seeking permanent, temporary, or contract work, leveraging these resources can help you navigate the job market, explore new opportunities, and advance your career in technology. Remember, recruiters and staffing agencies are there to support you, so make the most of their expertise and connections to achieve your career goals.

Chapter 16: Freelancing and Contract Work in Technology

In the ever-evolving world of technology, freelancing, and contract work offer unique opportunities for those seeking flexibility, independence, and variety in their careers. Unlike traditional full-time roles, freelancing and contract positions allow you to work on a project-by-project basis, giving you the freedom to choose the projects you want to work on and the clients you want to work with. This chapter will explore the ins and outs of freelancing and contract work in technology, providing you with a comprehensive guide to navigating this dynamic career path.

The Rise of Freelancing and Contract Work
Freelancing and contract work have become increasingly popular in the tech industry. With

the rise of remote work and the gig economy, many technology professionals are opting for these flexible work arrangements. This shift is driven by various factors, including the desire for better work-life balance, the opportunity to work on diverse projects, and the potential for higher earnings.

Freelancing allows you to be your own boss, set your own hours, and choose the projects that align with your interests and skills. Contract work, on the other hand, typically involves working for a company or client on a temporary basis, often for a specific project or duration. Both paths offer distinct advantages and challenges, making it important to understand what each entails.

Getting Started as a Freelancer or Contractor

Starting a freelancing or contract career in technology requires careful planning and preparation. Here are the key steps to getting started:

1. Identify Your Niche: Determine your area of expertise within technology. This could be software development, web design, data analysis, cybersecurity, or any other tech field. Specializing in a niche can help you stand out and attract clients looking for specific skills.

2. Build a Strong Portfolio: Create a portfolio that showcases your skills, past projects, and accomplishments. Your portfolio should highlight your best work and demonstrate your expertise to potential clients or employers. Include case studies, project summaries, and any relevant metrics or outcomes.

3. Set Up Your Business: As a freelancer or contractor, you'll need to manage your own business operations. This includes setting up a business structure (such as a sole proprietorship or LLC), managing finances, and handling taxes. Consider consulting with a financial advisor or accountant to ensure you're meeting all legal and financial requirements.

4. Establish Your Brand: Develop a professional brand that reflects your skills and expertise. This includes creating a website, designing a logo, and crafting a compelling personal statement or bio. Your brand should communicate what you offer and why clients should choose you.

5. Market Yourself: Promote your services through various channels, such as social media, online job boards, and freelance platforms like Upwork, Freelancer, or Toptal. Networking is also crucial; attend industry events, join tech communities, and connect with potential clients and other professionals in your field.

6. Set Your Rates: Determine how much to charge for your services. Research industry rates for your niche and consider factors such as your experience, skills, and the complexity of the projects. Be transparent with clients about your rates and any additional costs.

Finding Clients and Projects

Securing clients and projects is a key aspect of freelancing and contract work. Here are some strategies to help you find opportunities:

1. Utilize Online Platforms: Many freelance and contract opportunities are listed on online platforms and job boards. Create profiles on sites like LinkedIn, Upwork, and Freelancer to showcase your skills and connect with potential clients.

2. Network Actively: Leverage your professional network to find job leads and referrals. Reach out to former colleagues, industry contacts, and other professionals who may know of available opportunities or be willing to recommend you to their network.

3. Join Professional Groups: Participate in tech-related groups, forums, and communities where you can network with other professionals and potential clients. Being active in these communities can help you stay informed about job openings and industry trends.

4. Pitch Your Services: Proactively reach out to companies or clients you're interested in working with. Craft personalized proposals or pitches that highlight how your skills and experience align with their needs.

5. Build Relationships: Establish strong relationships with clients by delivering high-quality work and maintaining clear communication. Satisfied clients are more likely to provide repeat business and referrals.

Managing Freelance and Contract Work
Successfully managing your freelancing or contract work involves balancing multiple projects and clients while maintaining a high level of professionalism. Here are some tips to help you manage your workload:

1. Organize Your Projects: Use project management tools to keep track of deadlines, tasks, and progress. Tools like Trello, Asana, or

Monday.com can help you stay organized and manage your workload effectively.

2. Communicate Clearly: Maintain clear and regular communication with your clients. Provide updates on project progress, address any issues promptly, and ensure that you understand their expectations and requirements.

3. Manage Your Time: Time management is crucial for freelancers and contractors. Set a schedule that allows you to balance multiple projects and maintain a healthy work-life balance. Use time-tracking tools to monitor how much time you spend on each project.

4. Handle Contracts and Payments: Draft clear contracts that outline the scope of work, deadlines, payment terms, and any other relevant details. Use invoicing tools to manage payments and ensure timely billing. Consider setting up a system for tracking expenses and managing your finances.

5. Maintain Professionalism: Treat freelancing and contract work as a professional business. Meet deadlines, deliver high-quality work, and maintain a professional demeanor in all your interactions. Building a reputation for reliability and excellence will help you attract and retain clients.

Navigating Challenges in Freelancing and Contract Work

Freelancing and contract work come with their own set of challenges. Being prepared to address these challenges can help you succeed in your career:

1. Income Stability: Freelancers and contractors often face fluctuations in income. Plan for periods of low income by saving a portion of your earnings and creating a financial cushion.

2. Finding Clients: It can sometimes be challenging to find new clients or projects. Continuously market yourself, build

relationships, and diversify your sources of income to mitigate this challenge.

3. Managing Workload: Balancing multiple projects and clients can be demanding. Develop strong organizational skills, prioritize tasks, and set realistic deadlines to manage your workload effectively.

4. Legal and Tax Issues: Freelancers and contractors are responsible for their own taxes and legal obligations. Stay informed about tax laws and regulations, and consider working with a tax professional to ensure compliance.

5. Professional Isolation: Working independently can sometimes feel isolating. Stay connected with other professionals through networking events, online communities, and industry groups to combat loneliness and stay engaged with the industry.

Growing Your Freelance or Contract Career

As you gain experience and build your reputation, there are opportunities to grow your freelancing or contract career:

1. Expand Your Skill Set: Continuously update and expand your skills to stay competitive in the industry. Pursue additional training, certifications, or education to enhance your expertise.

2. Increase Your Rates: As you gain experience and establish a strong track record, consider increasing your rates to reflect your growing value and expertise.

3. Build a Team: If you find yourself overwhelmed with work, consider collaborating with other freelancers or hiring additional help. Building a team can help you take on larger projects and increase your capacity.

4. Explore New Markets: Look for opportunities to enter new markets or industries. Diversifying your client base and project types can help you

grow your business and reduce reliance on a single source of income.

5. Seek Long-Term Contracts: While freelancing and contract work often involve short-term projects, you may also seek long-term contracts or retainer agreements with clients. These arrangements can provide more stable income and ongoing work.

Freelancing and contract work in technology offer exciting opportunities for those who value flexibility, independence, and variety in their careers. By understanding the dynamics of freelancing and contract work, preparing effectively, and navigating the challenges, you can build a successful and fulfilling career in the tech industry. Whether you're drawn to the freedom of freelancing or the structured nature of contract work, embracing these paths can lead to new experiences, professional growth, and the chance to shape your career on your own terms.

Chapter 17: Continuing Education and Professional Development in IT

In the fast-paced world of technology, staying current with the latest advancements and continuously improving your skills is essential for career growth and success. Technology evolves rapidly, and what you know today might become outdated tomorrow. That's why ongoing education and professional development are crucial for anyone working in IT. This chapter explores why continuing education is important, how to pursue it effectively, and how to make the most of your professional development efforts.

The Importance of Continuing Education

In the IT field, technology changes constantly. New programming languages, software tools, and methodologies emerge regularly. Keeping your skills updated ensures that you remain relevant and competitive in the job market. Additionally, continuing education helps you adapt to changes and seize new opportunities that arise as technology evolves.

Continuous learning also contributes to personal growth. It allows you to explore new interests, develop new skills, and stay engaged in your work. This can lead to increased job satisfaction, better performance, and greater career advancement.

Exploring Different Learning Opportunities

There are various ways to pursue continuing education and professional development in IT. Here are some common options:

1. Online Courses: Online platforms like Coursera, Udemy, and LinkedIn Learning offer a wide range of courses on various tech topics.

These courses are often created by industry experts and can be taken at your own pace.

2. Certifications: Obtaining certifications from reputable organizations can enhance your credentials and demonstrate your expertise in specific areas. Popular certifications include CompTIA A+, Cisco CCNA, and Microsoft Certified Solutions Expert (MCSE).

3. Workshops and Seminars: Attending workshops and seminars provides hands-on experience and opportunities to learn from experts. These events often cover emerging technologies and industry trends.

4. Conferences: Technology conferences bring together professionals from around the world to discuss the latest advancements and network with peers. Conferences such as Google I/O, Microsoft Ignite, and AWS re: Invent offer valuable learning experiences.

5. University Programs: Many universities offer continuing education programs, including online degrees and specialized certificates in IT. These programs provide in-depth knowledge and academic credentials.

6. Professional Associations: Joining professional associations, such as the Association for Computing Machinery (ACM) or the Information Systems Audit and Control Association (ISACA), can provide access to resources, networking opportunities, and professional development events.

7. Books and Journals: Reading books and academic journals on technology topics can help you stay informed about new developments and deepen your understanding of specific areas.

Setting Learning Goals
To make the most of your continuing education efforts, it's important to set clear and achievable goals. Start by identifying what you want to achieve:

1. Career Objectives: Consider your long-term career goals. Are you aiming for a promotion, a career change, or the development of a new skill set? Your learning goals should align with your career objectives.

2. Skill Gaps: Evaluate your current skills and identify any gaps. Determine which areas you need to improve or update to stay competitive in your field.

3. Personal Interests: Pursue areas of technology that interest you. Learning about topics you're passionate about can make the process more enjoyable and engaging.

4. Industry Trends: Stay informed about industry trends and emerging technologies. Focus on learning about areas that are gaining traction and will likely be important in the future.

Creating a Learning Plan

Developing a structured learning plan can help you stay organized and motivated. Here's how to create an effective plan:

1. Choose Learning Resources: Select the courses, certifications, or other resources that best fit your learning goals. Consider factors such as content quality, cost, and delivery format.

2. Set a Timeline: Establish a timeline for completing your learning activities. Set deadlines for finishing courses, obtaining certifications, or achieving specific milestones.

3. Allocate Time: Dedicate regular time for learning. Whether it's an hour a day or a few hours each week, consistent effort will help you make steady progress.

4. Track Your Progress: Keep track of your progress and achievements. Use a journal or digital tool to monitor your learning activities, completed courses, and certifications.

5. Adjust as Needed: Be flexible and adjust your plan as needed. If you discover new interests or your career goals change, modify your learning plan to reflect these updates.

Balancing Learning with Work

Balancing your education and professional responsibilities can be challenging. Here are some tips to help you manage both:

1. Prioritize Learning: Set clear priorities and allocate time for learning that fits within your work schedule. Make learning a part of your routine to ensure consistent progress.

2. Integrate Learning into Work: Apply what you learn directly to your job. This not only reinforces your new skills but also demonstrates your commitment to professional growth to your employer.

3. Seek Support: If possible, discuss your learning goals with your employer. Some

companies offer support for continuing education, including financial assistance or flexible work arrangements.

4. Stay Organized: Use organizational tools to manage your time and keep track of both work and learning commitments. This can help you stay on top of deadlines and maintain a balance.

5. Take Breaks: Avoid burnout by taking regular breaks. Balancing work, learning, and personal time is crucial for maintaining productivity and well-being.

Evaluating the Impact of Your Learning
Assessing the impact of your continuing education efforts is important to ensure that your investments are paying off. Here's how to evaluate your progress:

1. Measure Skill Improvement: Reflect on how your new skills have enhanced your job performance or contributed to achieving your

career goals. Consider feedback from colleagues or supervisors.

2. Track Career Advancement: Monitor any career advancements, such as promotions or new job opportunities, that may result from your continued learning efforts.

3. Review Learning Outcomes: Evaluate the outcomes of the courses, certifications, or programs you've completed. Determine if they met your expectations and contributed to your professional development.

4. Seek Feedback: Request feedback from peers or mentors on your growth and development. Their perspectives can provide valuable insights into the effectiveness of your learning.

Staying Motivated
Maintaining motivation for continuing education can be challenging, especially with a busy schedule. Here are some strategies to stay motivated:

1. Set Short-Term Goals: Break your learning objectives into smaller, manageable goals. Achieving these short-term goals can provide a sense of accomplishment and keep you motivated.

2. Reward Yourself: Celebrate your achievements and milestones. Treat yourself to something enjoyable as a reward for completing courses or reaching learning goals.

3. Stay Engaged: Find ways to make learning enjoyable. Join study groups, participate in online forums, or engage with others who share your interests.

4. Remind Yourself of the Benefits: Keep in mind the benefits of continuing education, such as career advancement, personal growth, and staying up-to-date with technology. Reminding yourself of these benefits can help you stay focused and motivated.

Continuing education and professional development are vital for anyone working in IT. By staying current with technological advancements and continuously improving your skills, you can enhance your career prospects, adapt to industry changes, and achieve personal growth. Whether you pursue online courses, certifications, workshops, or other learning opportunities, maintaining a commitment to education will help you stay competitive and successful in the ever-evolving world of technology. Embrace the journey of lifelong learning, and let it drive your career forward in exciting and fulfilling ways.

Chapter 18: Remote Work Opportunities in Tech

Remote work has become a significant trend in the technology industry, offering tech professionals the flexibility to work from anywhere in the world. This shift towards remote work has been driven by advancements in technology, changing work preferences, and the global nature of the tech industry. This chapter explores the benefits and challenges of remote work in tech, the types of remote opportunities available, and how to effectively navigate a remote work environment.

The Rise of Remote Work in Tech
The concept of remote work, or telecommuting, has been around for a while, but it gained tremendous traction in recent years. For many tech professionals, working remotely is not just a

temporary solution but a preferred way of working. The rise of cloud computing, collaboration tools, and high-speed internet has made it possible for individuals to work efficiently from various locations.

Remote work in tech offers numerous advantages. It allows for greater flexibility, enabling employees to create a work environment that suits their personal needs and preferences. It also eliminates the need for commuting, saving time and reducing stress. For employers, remote work can lead to increased productivity, access to a global talent pool, and cost savings related to office space and overhead.

Types of Remote Tech Jobs

Remote work opportunities in tech span a wide range of roles and industries. Here are some common types of remote tech jobs:

1. Software Development: Software developers and engineers often work remotely, writing code, building applications, and collaborating

with teams using online tools. This role requires strong programming skills and the ability to work independently.

2. Web Development: Web developers create and maintain websites and web applications. This role involves working with various programming languages, frameworks, and design tools, and it can be performed from virtually anywhere.

3. Data Analysis: Data analysts collect, process, and interpret data to help businesses make informed decisions. With the right software and access to data sources, this role is well-suited for remote work.

4. IT Support: IT support specialists assist users with technical issues, troubleshoot problems, and provide solutions. Many IT support roles can be handled remotely through phone, chat, or remote access tools.

5. Cybersecurity: Cybersecurity professionals work to protect systems and data from security threats. They often analyze vulnerabilities, monitor networks, and implement security measures from remote locations.

6. Project Management: Tech project managers oversee the planning, execution, and completion of technology projects. They coordinate with remote teams, manage timelines, and ensure that project goals are met.

7. UX/UI Design: User experience (UX) and user interface (UI) designers focus on creating intuitive and visually appealing designs for applications and websites. This work can be done remotely using design software and collaboration tools.

8. Technical Writing: Technical writers create documentation, manuals, and guides for software and technology products. This role involves writing and editing content, which can be done from anywhere.

Finding Remote Tech Jobs
Finding remote tech jobs requires a proactive approach and the use of various resources. Here's how to find remote opportunities:

1. Job Boards and Websites: Many job boards specialize in remote work opportunities. Websites like Remote.co, We Work Remotely, and FlexJobs list remote tech positions across different industries.

2. Company Websites: Many tech companies offer remote work options. Check the career pages of companies you're interested in to find remote job listings and apply directly.

3. Professional Networks: Leverage your professional network to find remote job opportunities. Connect with former colleagues, attend industry events, and join online communities related to your field.

4. Freelance Platforms: Platforms like Upwork, Freelancer, and Toptal connect freelancers with clients seeking remote tech services. These platforms offer a range of project-based work and long-term contracts.

5. Social Media: Follow tech companies and industry leaders on social media platforms like LinkedIn and Twitter. Many organizations post remote job openings and updates about their remote work policies.

6. Remote Work Aggregators: Some websites and apps aggregate remote job listings from various sources. Tools like Remotive and Remote OK can help you find remote tech positions quickly.

Preparing for Remote Work

Success in a remote work environment requires preparation and the right mindset. Here's how to prepare for remote work:

1. Create a Dedicated Workspace: Set up a comfortable and productive workspace at home. Ensure you have the necessary equipment, such as a computer, high-speed internet, and any software required for your job.

2. Develop Self-Discipline: Working remotely requires strong self-discipline and time management skills. Establish a routine, set clear work hours, and avoid distractions to stay productive.

3. Use Collaboration Tools: Familiarize yourself with collaboration and communication tools such as Slack, Zoom, and Microsoft Teams. These tools help you stay connected with your team and manage projects effectively.

4. Set Goals and Priorities: Define your goals and priorities for each day or week. Creating a to-do list and setting deadlines can help you stay focused and organized.

5. Communicate Effectively: Clear communication is essential in a remote work environment. Keep your team informed about your progress, ask for feedback, and address any issues promptly.

6. Manage Your Well-being: Working remotely can sometimes lead to feelings of isolation. Make an effort to stay connected with colleagues, take regular breaks, and maintain a healthy work-life balance.

Overcoming Challenges in Remote Work
While remote work offers many benefits, it also comes with its own set of challenges. Here's how to overcome common remote work challenges:

1. Isolation: Working remotely can sometimes feel lonely. Combat isolation by staying engaged with your team through regular check-ins, virtual meetings, and social interactions.

2. Communication Barriers: Remote work can lead to communication challenges. Ensure you use clear and concise communication, and make use of video calls and chat tools to enhance interactions.

3. Time Zone Differences: Working with a distributed team may involve managing time zone differences. Coordinate meeting times that work for everyone and be mindful of overlapping work hours.

4. Distractions: Home environments can be filled with distractions. Set boundaries with family or housemates, and create a dedicated workspace to minimize interruptions.

5. Technology Issues: Technical problems can arise while working remotely. Ensure you have a reliable internet connection, keep your software up-to-date, and have a plan for troubleshooting common issues.

Balancing Work and Personal Life

Maintaining a healthy work-life balance is crucial for remote workers. Here's how to achieve balance while working remotely:

1. Set Boundaries: Establish clear boundaries between work and personal time. Define your work hours and stick to them to avoid overworking or blending work with personal activities.

2. Take Breaks: Regular breaks are important for productivity and well-being. Schedule short breaks throughout the day to rest, recharge, and avoid burnout.

3. Use Technology Wisely: While technology facilitates remote work, it can also blur the lines between work and personal life. Set limits on checking work emails or messages outside of work hours.

4. Create a Routine: Develop a daily routine that includes time for work, exercise, meals, and

relaxation. A structured routine can help you stay organized and maintain a healthy balance.

5. Engage in Activities: Pursue hobbies, exercise, and spend time with family and friends to maintain a balanced life. Engaging in non-work activities can help reduce stress and improve overall well-being.

Growing in a Remote Work Environment
Remote work can offer significant career growth opportunities if approached with the right mindset. Here's how to grow professionally while working remotely:

1. Seek Feedback: Regularly seek feedback from your manager and colleagues. Constructive feedback helps you improve your skills and performance, contributing to career advancement.

2. Pursue Professional Development: Take advantage of online courses, webinars, and certifications to enhance your skills and

knowledge. Continuous learning can help you stay competitive and advance in your career.

3. Build Relationships: Cultivate relationships with your remote team and other professionals in your industry. Networking and building connections can lead to new opportunities and career growth.

4. Demonstrate Initiative: Show initiative by taking on new projects, suggesting improvements, and contributing to team goals. Proactive behavior can lead to recognition and career advancement.

5. Stay Updated: Keep up with industry trends, technological advancements, and best practices. Staying informed helps you remain relevant and contributes to your professional growth.

Remote work in tech offers incredible opportunities for flexibility, independence, and career growth. By understanding the benefits and challenges, preparing effectively, and navigating the remote work environment, you can build a successful and fulfilling career from anywhere in the world. Embrace the opportunities that remote work provides, stay motivated, and continue to develop your skills and professional network. With the right approach, remote work can be a rewarding and enriching experience that aligns with your career goals and personal preferences.

Chapter 19: Balancing Work and Life in a Tech Career

In the demanding world of technology, finding a balance between work and personal life can often feel challenging. The fast pace, constant innovation, and high expectations in tech careers can sometimes blur the lines between professional and personal time. However, maintaining a healthy balance is essential for both your well-being and long-term career success. This chapter explores practical strategies for achieving balance in your tech career, helping you manage your time effectively and enjoy a fulfilling life outside of work.

Understanding the Importance of Balance
A balanced life is crucial for overall happiness and productivity. When work takes up too much

of your time and energy, it can lead to stress, burnout, and dissatisfaction. On the other hand, neglecting your career responsibilities can hinder your professional growth and job performance. Striking a balance between work and personal life helps you stay motivated, reduce stress, and improve your overall quality of life.

Setting Boundaries
One of the first steps to achieving work-life balance is setting clear boundaries between your professional and personal life. This involves:

Creating a Dedicated Workspace: Having a specific area where you work helps to separate work from home life. If you work from home, try to set up a space that is solely for work purposes, making it easier to switch off when the workday ends.

Defining Work Hours: Establish clear work hours and stick to them. Communicate your availability to colleagues and managers to set expectations. Avoid checking work emails or taking work calls outside of these hours.

Managing Availability: If you're in a role that requires frequent communication, consider setting specific times for checking emails and messages. This helps prevent constant interruptions and allows you to focus on personal activities.

Prioritizing Tasks

Effective time management is key to balancing work and personal life. Here's how to prioritize tasks effectively:

Identify Priorities: Start by listing your work and personal tasks. Identify which ones are most important and need immediate attention. This helps you focus on what truly matters and avoid getting overwhelmed by less critical tasks.

Use a Planner: Utilize a planner or digital calendar to organize your schedule. Set deadlines for tasks and allocate specific times for work and personal activities. This helps you stay organized and ensures you have time for both.

Break Tasks into Smaller Steps: Large projects can seem daunting. Break them into smaller, manageable tasks and tackle them one step at a time. This makes it easier to progress without feeling overwhelmed.

Avoid Multitasking: While it might seem efficient, multitasking can actually decrease productivity. Focus on one task at a time to ensure quality work and avoid distractions.

Incorporating Breaks and Downtime
Regular breaks and downtime are essential for maintaining productivity and preventing burnout. Here's how to incorporate them into your routine:

Take Regular Breaks: During work hours, schedule short breaks to rest and recharge. Step away from your desk, stretch, or take a walk.

This helps maintain focus and energy throughout the day.

Use Vacation Time: Take advantage of vacation days to disconnect from work and recharge. A change of scenery and time away from work responsibilities can help you return with renewed energy and perspective.

Engage in Hobbies: Pursue activities that you enjoy outside of work. Whether it's reading, exercising, or spending time with family and friends, engaging in hobbies helps you relax and maintain a balanced life.

Practice Mindfulness: Incorporate mindfulness techniques, such as meditation or deep breathing exercises, into your daily routine. Mindfulness helps manage stress and improves overall well-being.

Managing Work-Related Stress
Tech careers can be high-pressure and stressful. Here's how to manage stress effectively:

Recognize Stress Triggers: Identify what causes you stress at work. It could be tight deadlines, high expectations, or challenging projects. Understanding these triggers helps you address them more effectively.

Develop Stress-Relief Strategies: Find healthy ways to manage stress. This could include physical activities like exercise, relaxation techniques, or talking to a mentor or counselor.

Seek Support: Don't hesitate to seek support if you're feeling overwhelmed. Talk to your manager about workload concerns or explore resources offered by your company, such as employee assistance programs.

Maintain a Positive Outlook: Focus on what you can control and approach challenges with a positive attitude. A constructive mindset helps you handle stress better and stay resilient in the face of difficulties.

Balancing Remote and On-Site Work

For those in hybrid or remote work settings, balancing work and life can present additional challenges. Here's how to manage these dynamics:

Create a Routine: Establish a daily routine that includes both work and personal activities. Consistent routines help you maintain structure and balance, regardless of where you're working.

Separate Work and Personal Spaces: If working from home, clearly distinguish between work and personal spaces. This helps you mentally switch between work and relaxation modes.

Set Clear Expectations: Communicate with your team and manager about your availability and work preferences. Clear communication helps prevent misunderstandings and ensures that your work-life balance is respected.

Stay Connected: Engage with colleagues and maintain social interactions to avoid isolation. Regular check-ins and virtual meetings help you stay connected and integrated with your team.

Evaluating and Adjusting Your Balance
Achieving work-life balance is an ongoing process. Regularly evaluate your balance and make adjustments as needed:

Reflect on Your Well-Being: Periodically assess how you're feeling about your work-life balance. Are you experiencing stress, burnout, or dissatisfaction? Use this reflection to identify areas for improvement.

Seek Feedback: Ask for feedback from colleagues, friends, or family about your work-life balance. They can provide insights and suggestions for adjustments.

Make Adjustments: Be willing to make changes to your routine or work habits if necessary.

Flexibility and adaptability are key to maintaining a healthy balance.

Celebrate Achievements: Recognize and celebrate your achievements, both at work and in your personal life. Acknowledging successes helps you stay motivated and appreciate the balance you've achieved.

Balancing work and life in a tech career is essential for maintaining overall well-being and achieving long-term success. By setting boundaries, managing your time effectively, incorporating breaks, and addressing stress, you can create a fulfilling and balanced life. Remember that achieving balance is a continuous process that requires regular evaluation and adjustments. Embrace the journey, stay mindful of your needs, and strive for a harmonious blend of professional and personal fulfillment. With the right approach, you can enjoy a rewarding career in tech while also nurturing a satisfying and balanced life outside of work.

Chapter 20: Future Trends in Technology and IT Careers

The world of technology is ever-evolving, with new innovations and trends continually reshaping the landscape. As we look towards the future, it's clear that technology and IT careers will experience significant changes, driven by advancements in technology and shifts in societal needs. Understanding these trends is crucial for anyone looking to navigate the future job market and make informed career decisions. This chapter explores some of the most important future trends in technology and IT careers, helping you prepare for the opportunities and challenges ahead.

The Rise of Artificial Intelligence and Machine Learning

Artificial Intelligence (AI) and Machine Learning (ML) are at the forefront of technological innovation. These technologies enable computers to learn from data and make decisions with minimal human intervention. As AI and ML continue to advance, they are expected to become integral to various industries, from healthcare and finance to transportation and entertainment.

AI and ML are transforming job roles and creating new opportunities. For instance, data scientists and AI specialists are in high demand to develop and manage AI systems. These professionals work on creating algorithms, training models, and analyzing data to make AI systems more accurate and effective. Additionally, AI is expected to enhance productivity by automating routine tasks, allowing workers to focus on more complex and creative aspects of their jobs.

Growth of Cybersecurity

As technology advances, so do the threats and vulnerabilities associated with it. Cybersecurity is becoming increasingly critical as organizations and individuals seek to protect their data and systems from cyberattacks. The growing number of data breaches and cyber incidents highlights the need for skilled cybersecurity professionals.

The demand for cybersecurity experts is expected to rise significantly. These professionals work on safeguarding networks, detecting and responding to threats, and implementing security measures to protect sensitive information. With the increasing complexity of cyber threats, cybersecurity roles will require advanced skills and knowledge, including expertise in areas such as encryption, threat analysis, and incident response.

Expansion of Cloud Computing

Cloud computing has revolutionized the way businesses store and manage data. It allows organizations to access computing resources over the internet, offering flexibility, scalability, and cost-efficiency. As more companies migrate to the cloud, the demand for cloud computing professionals is expected to grow.

Cloud architects, engineers, and administrators are needed to design, implement, and manage cloud-based solutions. These roles involve working with cloud platforms like Amazon Web Services (AWS), Microsoft Azure, and Google Cloud Platform (GCP). Cloud professionals must be skilled in managing cloud infrastructure, ensuring security, and optimizing performance. The shift to cloud computing also means that IT professionals will need to adapt to new tools and technologies.

Emergence of the Internet of Things (IoT)

The Internet of Things (IoT) refers to the growing network of interconnected devices that communicate and exchange data. From smart home devices to industrial sensors, IoT is expanding rapidly and has the potential to impact various aspects of daily life and business operations.

IoT creates new opportunities for tech professionals in areas such as device development, data analysis, and system integration. IoT engineers work on creating and managing connected devices, while data analysts interpret the vast amounts of data generated by these devices. As IoT technology evolves, professionals will need to address challenges related to data privacy, security, and interoperability.

Evolution of 5G Technology

The rollout of 5G technology is set to revolutionize connectivity and communication. With faster speeds, lower latency, and increased capacity, 5G will enable new applications and services, such as enhanced virtual reality (VR), autonomous vehicles, and smart cities.

As 5G technology becomes more widespread, there will be a growing need for professionals who can design, implement, and maintain 5G networks. Network engineers, telecommunications specialists, and IoT developers will play a key role in leveraging 5G to create innovative solutions and applications. Additionally, the expansion of 5G will drive demand for new tools and technologies that support high-speed connectivity.

Rise of Remote Work and Virtual Collaboration
The COVID-19 pandemic accelerated the adoption of remote work and virtual collaboration tools. As organizations recognize the benefits of flexible work arrangements, remote work is likely to remain a significant aspect of the modern workplace.

The future of remote work will involve advancements in virtual collaboration tools, such as video conferencing platforms, project management software, and virtual reality environments. IT professionals will need to develop and manage these tools, ensuring they are secure, reliable, and user-friendly. Additionally, remote work will continue to influence job roles and organizational structures, requiring new strategies for managing remote teams and maintaining productivity.

Development of Quantum Computing

Quantum computing represents a significant leap forward in computational power. Unlike traditional computers, which use bits to process information, quantum computers use qubits, allowing them to perform complex calculations at unprecedented speeds.

As quantum computing technology progresses, it has the potential to solve problems that are currently intractable for classical computers. This includes areas such as cryptography, drug discovery, and optimization problems. Quantum computing professionals will need to develop and apply algorithms, build quantum hardware, and explore new applications for this technology. The field is still in its early stages, offering exciting opportunities for those interested in cutting-edge technology.

Focus on Ethical Technology

As technology becomes more integrated into our lives, ethical considerations are gaining prominence. Issues such as data privacy, algorithmic bias, and the societal impact of technology are increasingly important.

The focus on ethical technology will lead to the development of new roles and responsibilities. Professionals will need to address ethical challenges, ensure compliance with regulations, and promote responsible technology use. This may involve working on data protection policies, developing fair and unbiased algorithms, and considering the broader implications of technology on society.

Skills for the Future
To thrive in the evolving tech landscape, professionals will need to develop a diverse set of skills. In addition to technical expertise, skills such as problem-solving, critical thinking, and adaptability will be essential. The ability to work with emerging technologies, stay current with industry trends, and continuously learn will be crucial for career success.

Soft skills, including communication, collaboration, and emotional intelligence, will also play a key role. As technology becomes more integrated with various aspects of work and life, the ability to work effectively with diverse teams, manage projects, and navigate complex situations will be highly valued.

The future of technology and IT careers is filled with exciting possibilities and challenges. By staying informed about emerging trends and developing relevant skills, you can position yourself for success in a rapidly changing field. Embrace the opportunities presented by advancements in AI, cybersecurity, cloud computing, IoT, 5G, quantum computing, and ethical technology. As you navigate your tech career, remember that adaptability, continuous learning, and a forward-thinking mindset will be your greatest assets in shaping a successful and fulfilling future.

Conclusion

Navigating the world of technology and IT can be both thrilling and challenging. As we have explored throughout this book, the tech industry is characterized by rapid change and continuous innovation. Whether you're just starting out or looking to advance your career, understanding the dynamics of this field is essential for making informed decisions and achieving success.

In this journey, you've learned about the key trends shaping the future of technology and IT careers. From the rise of artificial intelligence and machine learning to the growing importance of cybersecurity and the expansion of cloud computing, these trends highlight the ever-evolving nature of the tech industry. The emergence of the Internet of Things, the rollout of 5G technology, and the development of quantum computing further illustrate the boundless opportunities and challenges that lie ahead.

To thrive in this dynamic environment, it's crucial to develop both technical and soft skills. Embrace the need for continuous learning and stay updated with industry trends. Building a strong foundation in essential skills, such as programming, data analysis, and cybersecurity, will position you for success. Additionally, honing your abilities in communication, problem-solving, and adaptability will enhance your effectiveness and career prospects.

Balancing work and personal life is another critical aspect of a successful tech career. Setting clear boundaries, managing your time effectively, and incorporating breaks and downtime into your routine will help you maintain well-being and productivity. As remote work and virtual collaboration become more prevalent, developing strategies to navigate these work environments will be vital.

As you move forward in your tech career, remember that opportunities abound for those who are proactive, adaptable, and forward-thinking. Whether you are exploring new job roles, pursuing certifications, or considering freelance and contract work, stay focused on your goals and be open to new possibilities.

The future of technology and IT is bright, with endless potential for innovation and growth. By equipping yourself with the right skills, staying informed about industry trends, and maintaining a healthy work-life balance, you can confidently navigate the ever-changing landscape and achieve a fu
fulfilling and successful career in technology.

www.ingramcontent.com/pod-product-compliance
Lightning Source LLC
Chambersburg PA
CBHW071918210526
45479CB00002B/461